GRAPHIC BIOGRAPHIES

Christopher COLUMBUS
famous explorer

by Mary Dodson Wade

illustrated by

Rod Whigham and Charles Barnett III

Consultant:

Keith A. Pickering, Associate Editor
Dio: The International Journal of Scientific History

Capstone
press

Mankato, Minnesota

Graphic Library is published by Capstone Press,
151 Good Counsel Drive, P.O. Box 669, Mankato, Minnesota 56002.
www.capstonepub.com

Books published by Capstone Press are manufactured with paper
containing at least 10 percent post-consumer waste.

Library of Congress Cataloging-in-Publication Data
Wade, Mary Dodson.
    Christopher Columbus : famous explorer / by Mary Dodson Wade; illustrated by Rod
Whigham and Charles Barnett III.
    p. cm.—(Graphic library. Graphic biographies)
    Summary: "In graphic novel format, tells the life story of Christopher Columbus and his
discovery of the Americas"—Provided by publisher.
    Includes bibliographical references and index.
    Audience: Grades 4–6.
    ISBN–13: 978-0-7368-6853-2 (hardcover)
    ISBN–10: 0-7368-6853-4 (hardcover)
    ISBN–13: 978-0-7368-7905-7 (softcover pbk.)
    ISBN–10: 0-7368-7905-6 (softcover pbk.)
    1. Columbus, Christopher—Comic books, strips, etc.—Juvenile literature. 2. Explorers—
America—Biography—Comic books, strips, etc.—Juvenile literature. 3. Explorers—Spain—
Biography—Comic books, strips, etc.—Juvenile literature. 4. America—Discovery and
exploration—Spanish—Comic books, strips, etc.—Juvenile literature. 5. Graphic novels. I.
Whigham, Rod, 1954– II. Barnett, Charles, III. III. Title. IV. Series.
E111.W244 2007
970.01'5092—dc22   2006023793

Designers
Bob Lentz and Kyle Grenz

Colorist
Melissa Kaercher

Editor
Aaron Sautter

Editor's note: Direct quotations from primary sources are indicated by a yellow background.

Direct quotations appear on the following pages:
Pages 10, 11, 18, from *The Worlds of Christopher Columbus* by William D. Phillips, Jr. and
    Carla Rahn Phillips (New York: Cambridge University Press, 1992).
Page 21, from *The Life of the Admiral Christopher Columbus by His Son Ferdinand*
    by Fernando Colón, Translated by Benjamin Keen (New Brunswick, N.J.: Rutgers
    University Press, 1992).

Printed in the United States of America in Stevens Point, Wisconsin.
022011   006090R

Table of Contents

Chapter 1
Chasing a Dream

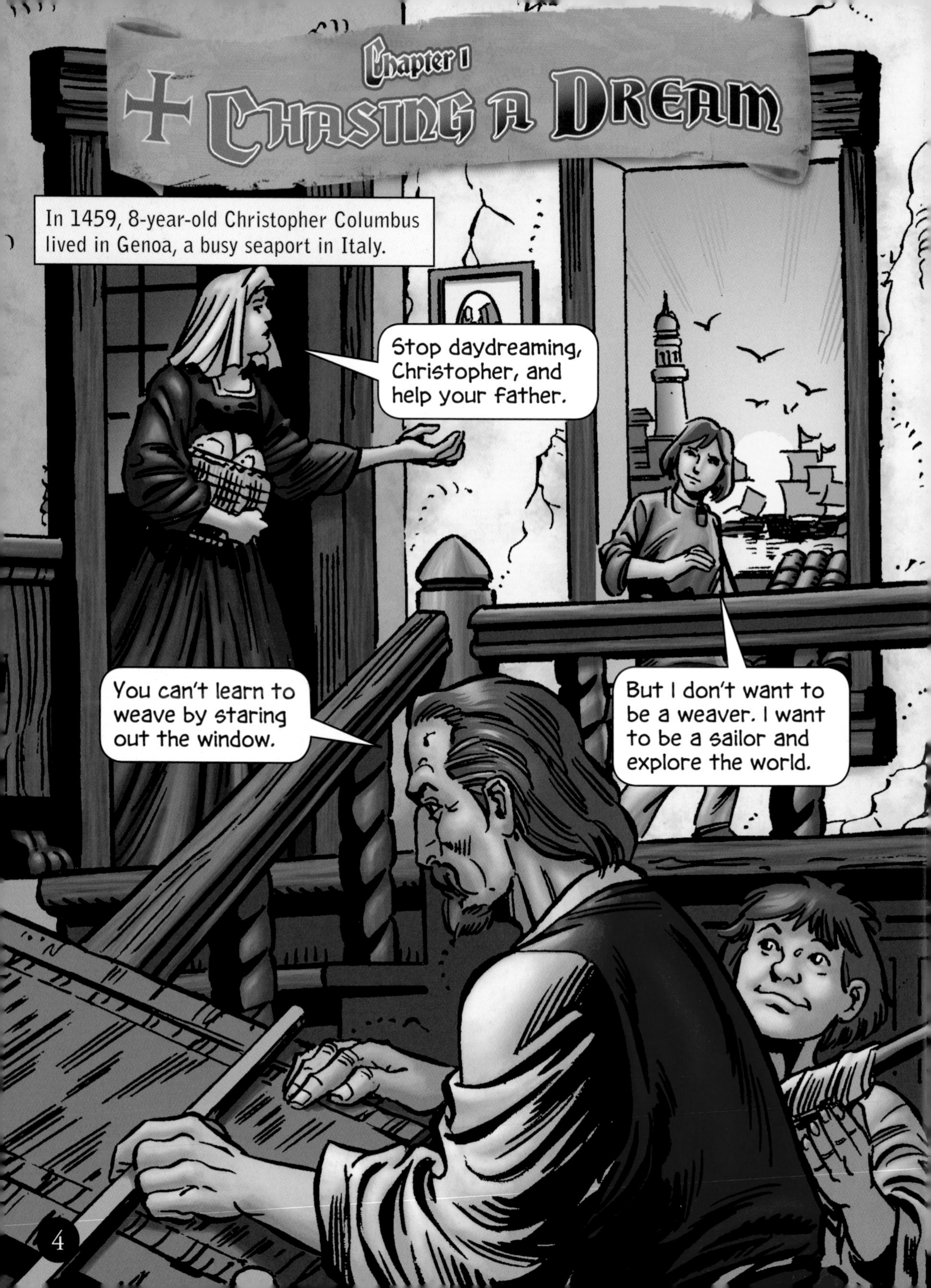

In 1459, 8-year-old Christopher Columbus lived in Genoa, a busy seaport in Italy.
Stop daydreaming, Christopher, and help your father.
You can't learn to weave by staring out the window.
But I don't want to be a weaver. I want to be a sailor and explore the world.

By age 14, Columbus' dream of becoming a sailor came true.

I'll do any job, sir.

I'm finally going to sea.

We need a ship's boy. You can tend the hourglass. Turn it just as the last grain of sand falls through.

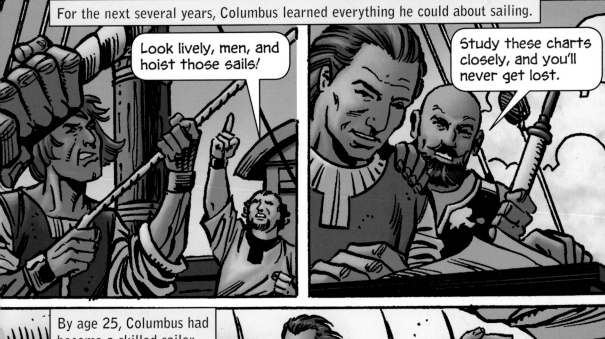

For the next several years, Columbus learned everything he could about sailing.

Look lively, men, and hoist those sails!

Study these charts closely, and you'll never get lost.

By age 25, Columbus had become a skilled sailor.

This wind and current will bring us home early.

5

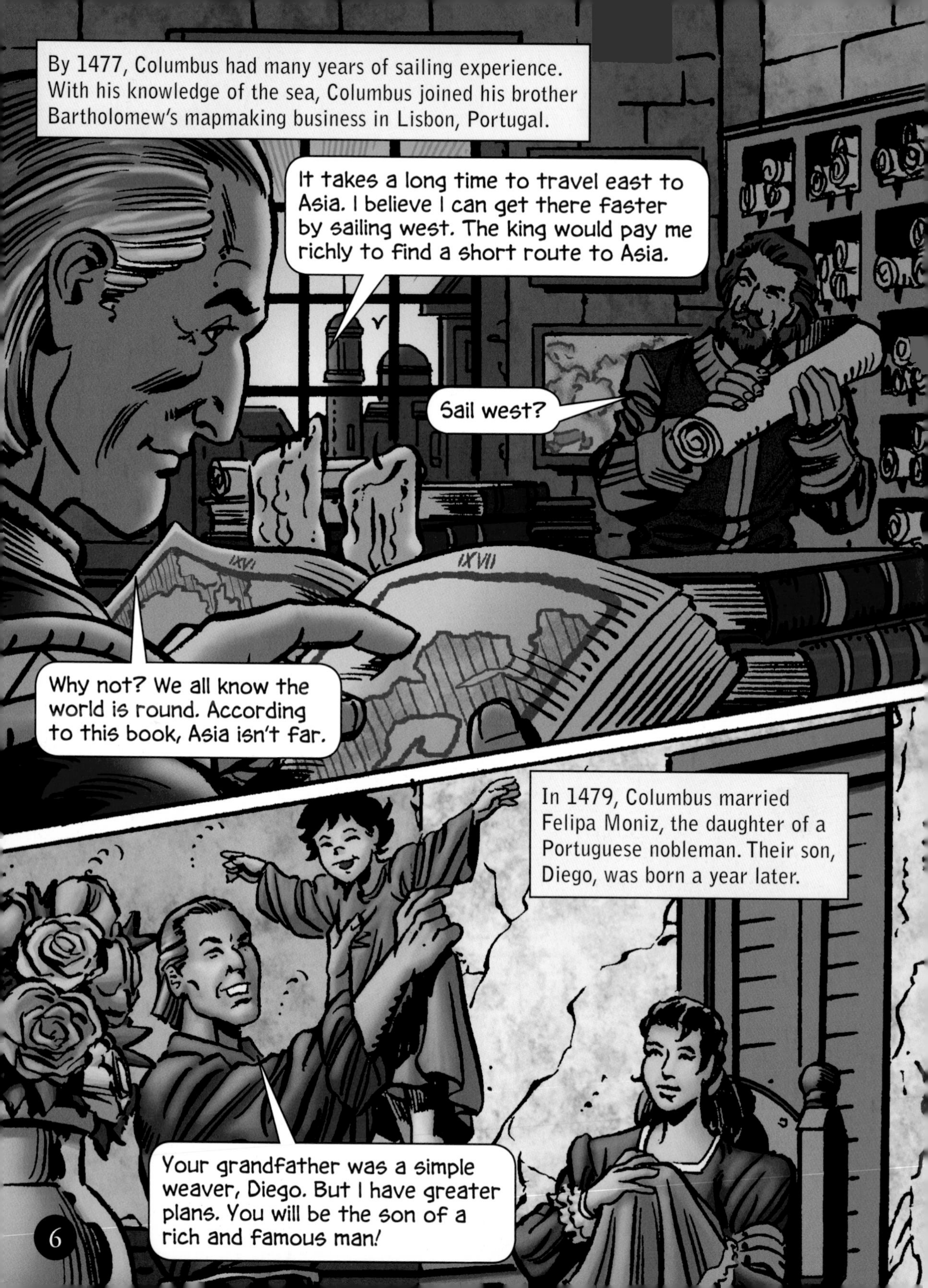

By 1477, Columbus had many years of sailing experience. With his knowledge of the sea, Columbus joined his brother Bartholomew's mapmaking business in Lisbon, Portugal.
It takes a long time to travel east to Asia. I believe I can get there faster by sailing west. The king would pay me richly to find a short route to Asia.
Sail west?
Why not? We all know the world is round. According to this book, Asia isn't far.
In 1479, Columbus married Felipa Moniz, the daughter of a Portuguese nobleman. Their son, Diego, was born a year later.
Your grandfather was a simple weaver, Diego. But I have greater plans. You will be the son of a rich and famous man!

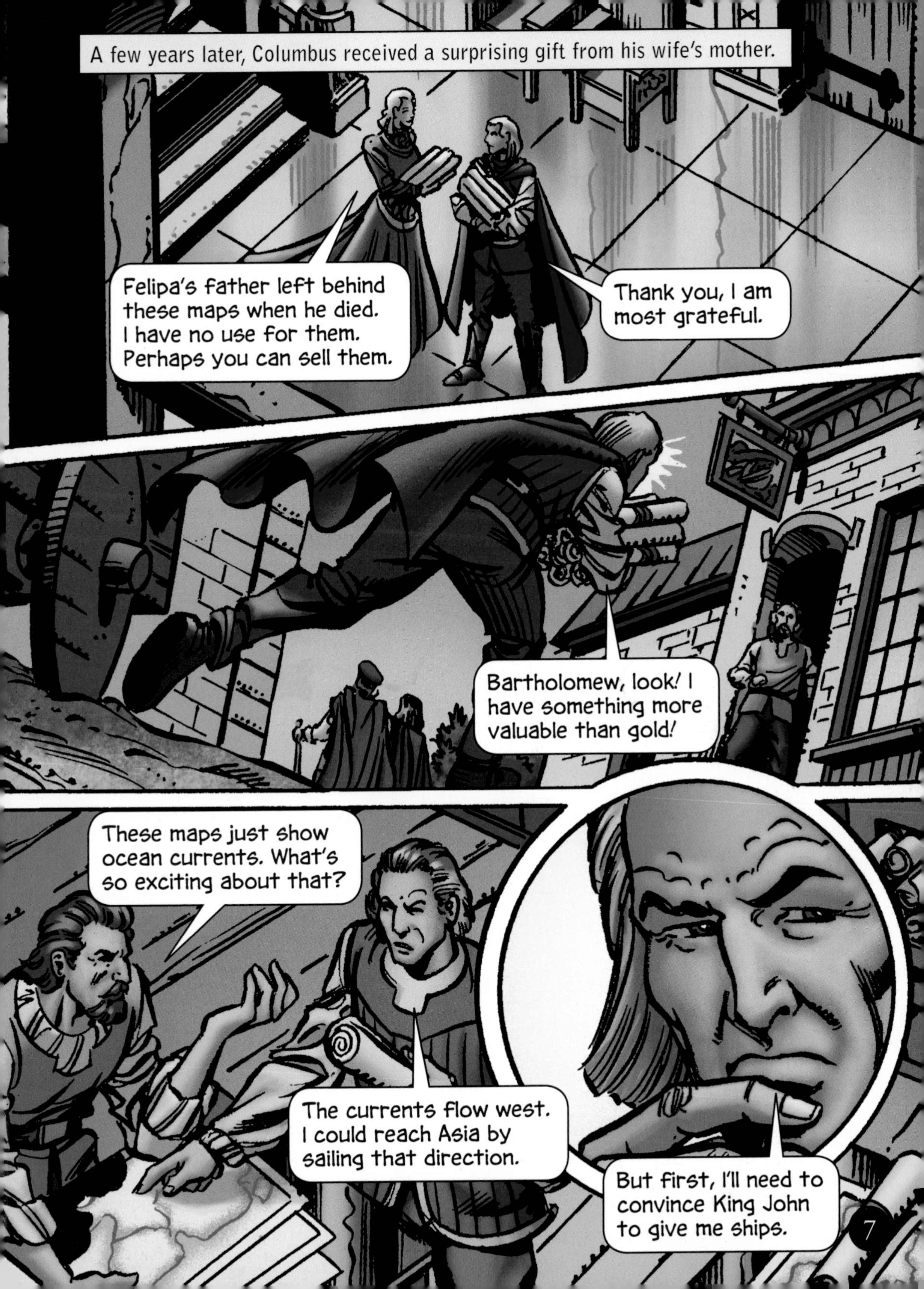
A few years later, Columbus received a surprising gift from his wife's mother.
Felipa's father left behind these maps when he died. I have no use for them. Perhaps you can sell them.
Thank you, I am most grateful.
Bartholomew, look! I have something more valuable than gold!
These maps just show ocean currents. What's so exciting about that?
The currents flow west. I could reach Asia by sailing that direction.
But first, I'll need to convince King John to give me ships.

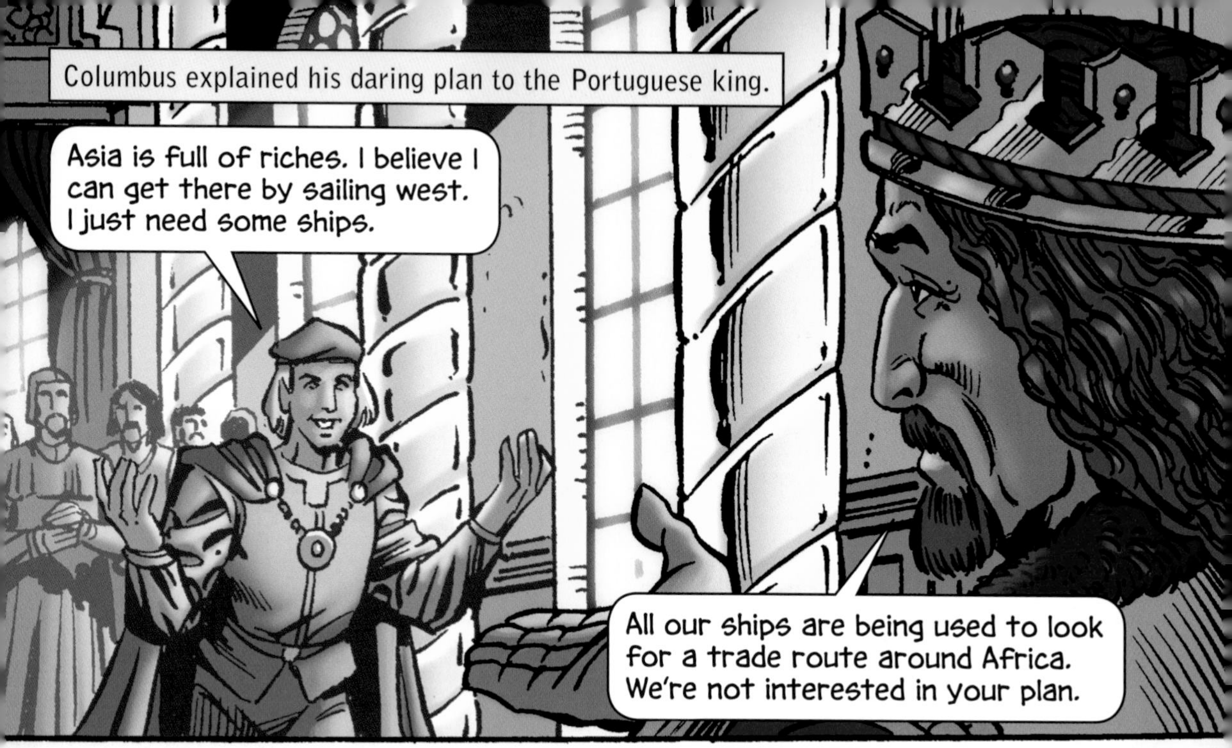
Columbus explained his daring plan to the Portuguese king.
Asia is full of riches. I believe I can get there by sailing west. I just need some ships.
All our ships are being used to look for a trade route around Africa. We're not interested in your plan.

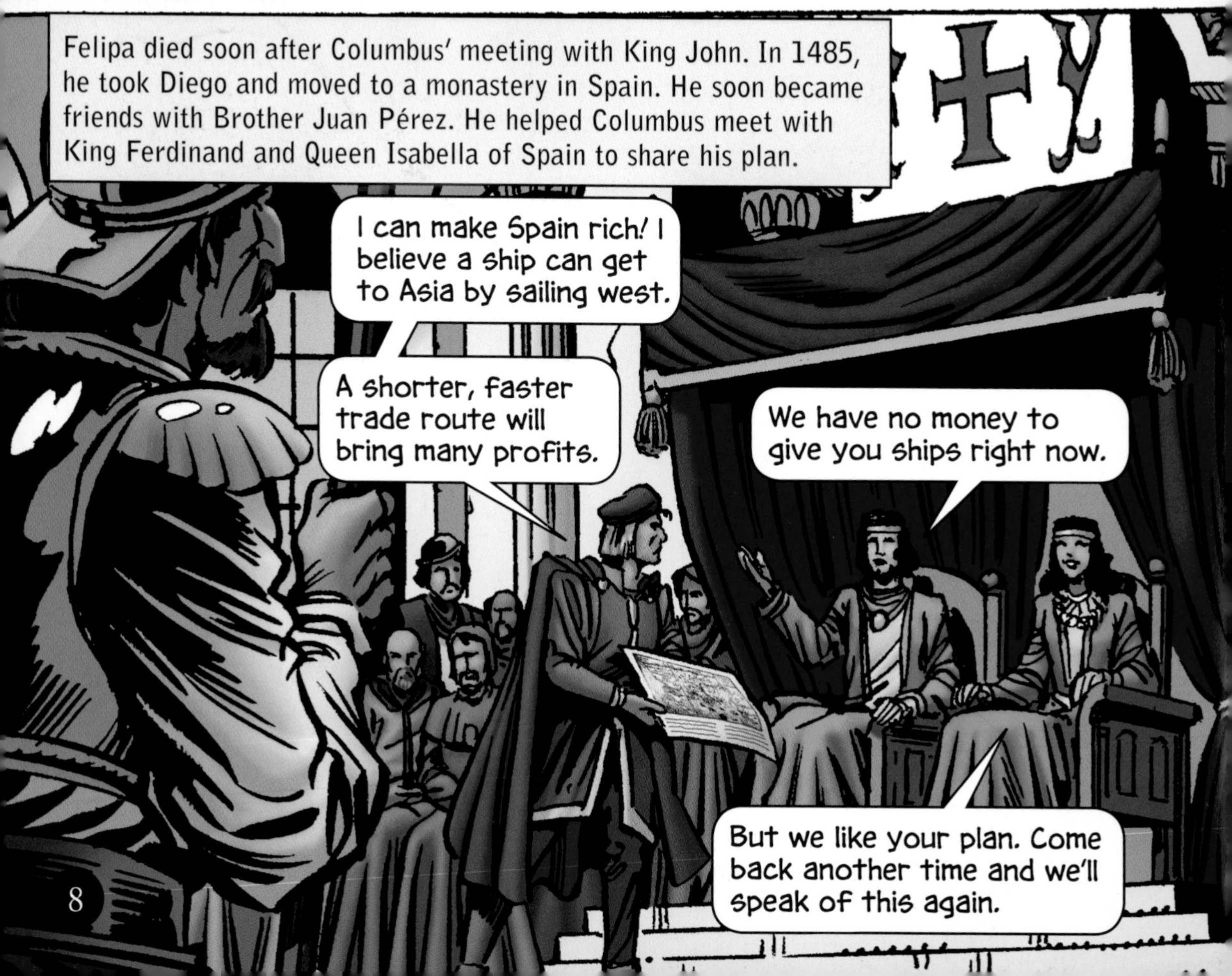
Felipa died soon after Columbus' meeting with King John. In 1485, he took Diego and moved to a monastery in Spain. He soon became friends with Brother Juan Pérez. He helped Columbus meet with King Ferdinand and Queen Isabella of Spain to share his plan.
I can make Spain rich! I believe a ship can get to Asia by sailing west.
A shorter, faster trade route will bring many profits.
We have no money to give you ships right now.
But we like your plan. Come back another time and we'll speak of this again.

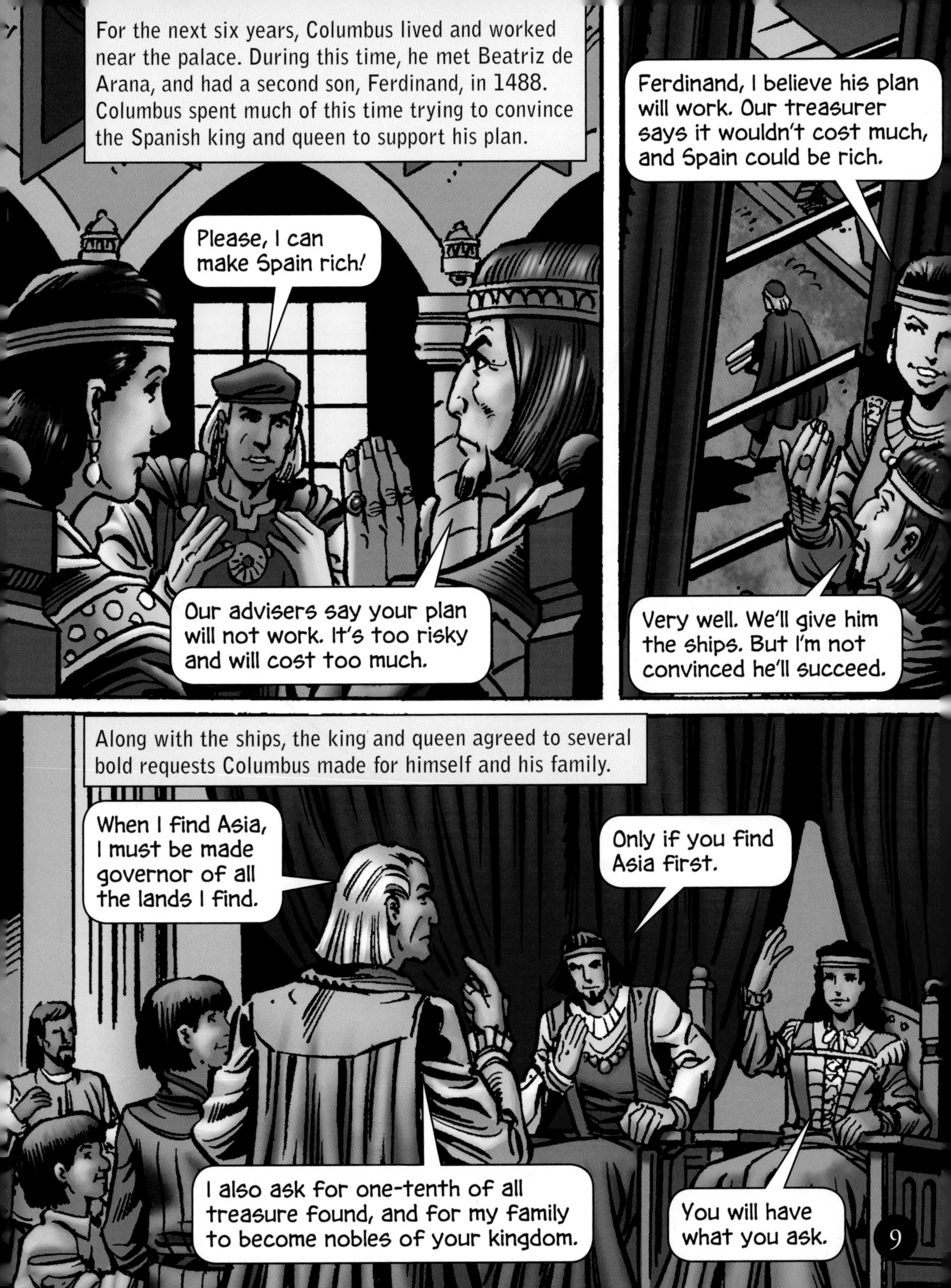

For the next six years, Columbus lived and worked near the palace. During this time, he met Beatriz de Arana, and had a second son, Ferdinand, in 1488. Columbus spent much of this time trying to convince the Spanish king and queen to support his plan.
Please, I can make Spain rich!
Our advisers say your plan will not work. It's too risky and will cost too much.
Ferdinand, I believe his plan will work. Our treasurer says it wouldn't cost much, and Spain could be rich.
Very well. We'll give him the ships. But I'm not convinced he'll succeed.
Along with the ships, the king and queen agreed to several bold requests Columbus made for himself and his family.
When I find Asia, I must be made governor of all the lands I find.
Only if you find Asia first.
I also ask for one-tenth of all treasure found, and for my family to become nobles of your kingdom.
You will have what you ask.

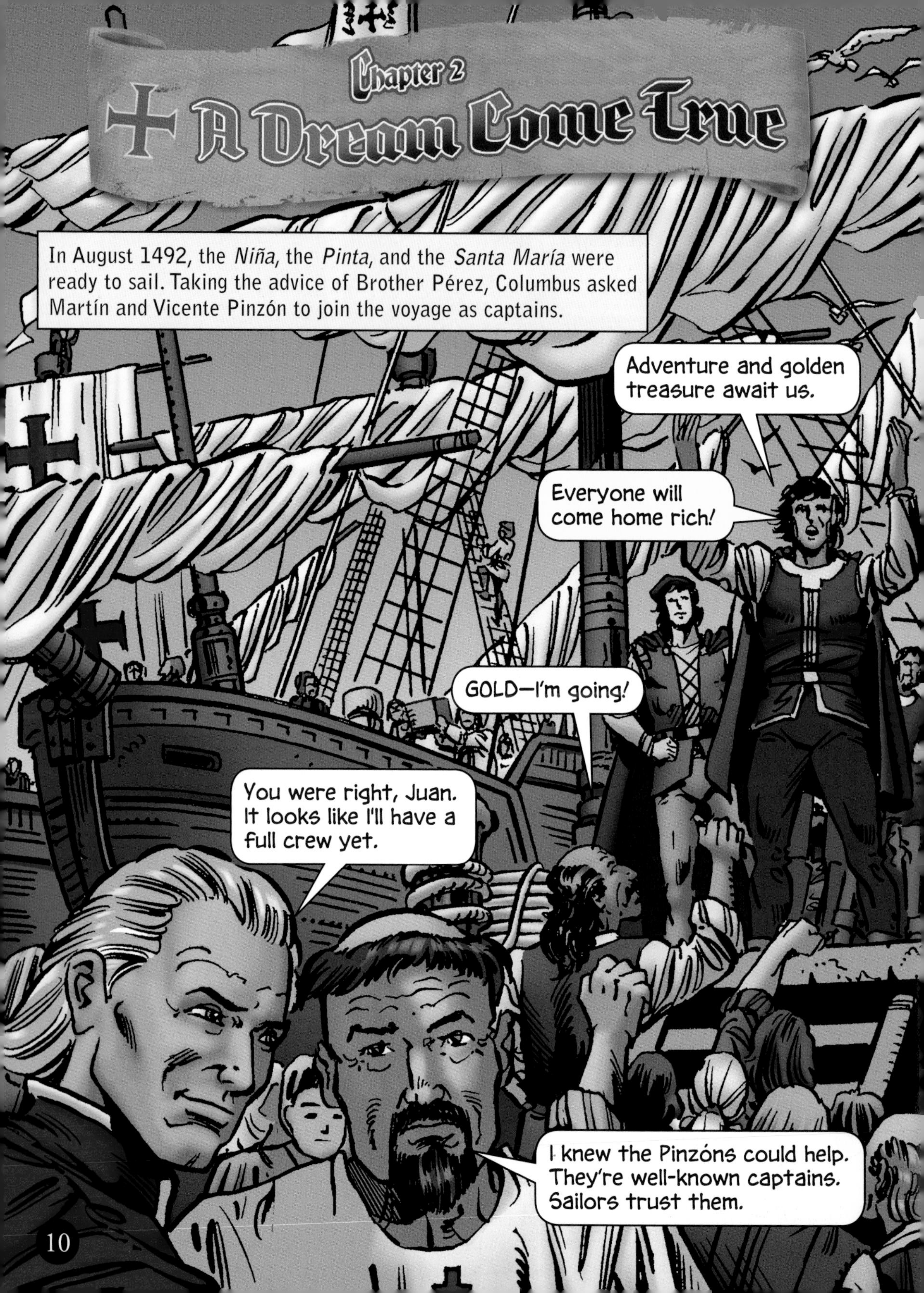

Chapter 2
A Dream Come True
In August 1492, the *Niña*, the *Pinta*, and the *Santa María* were ready to sail. Taking the advice of Brother Pérez, Columbus asked Martín and Vicente Pinzón to join the voyage as captains.
Adventure and golden treasure await us.
Everyone will come home rich!
GOLD—I'm going!
You were right, Juan. It looks like I'll have a full crew yet.
I knew the Pinzóns could help. They're well-known captains. Sailors trust them.

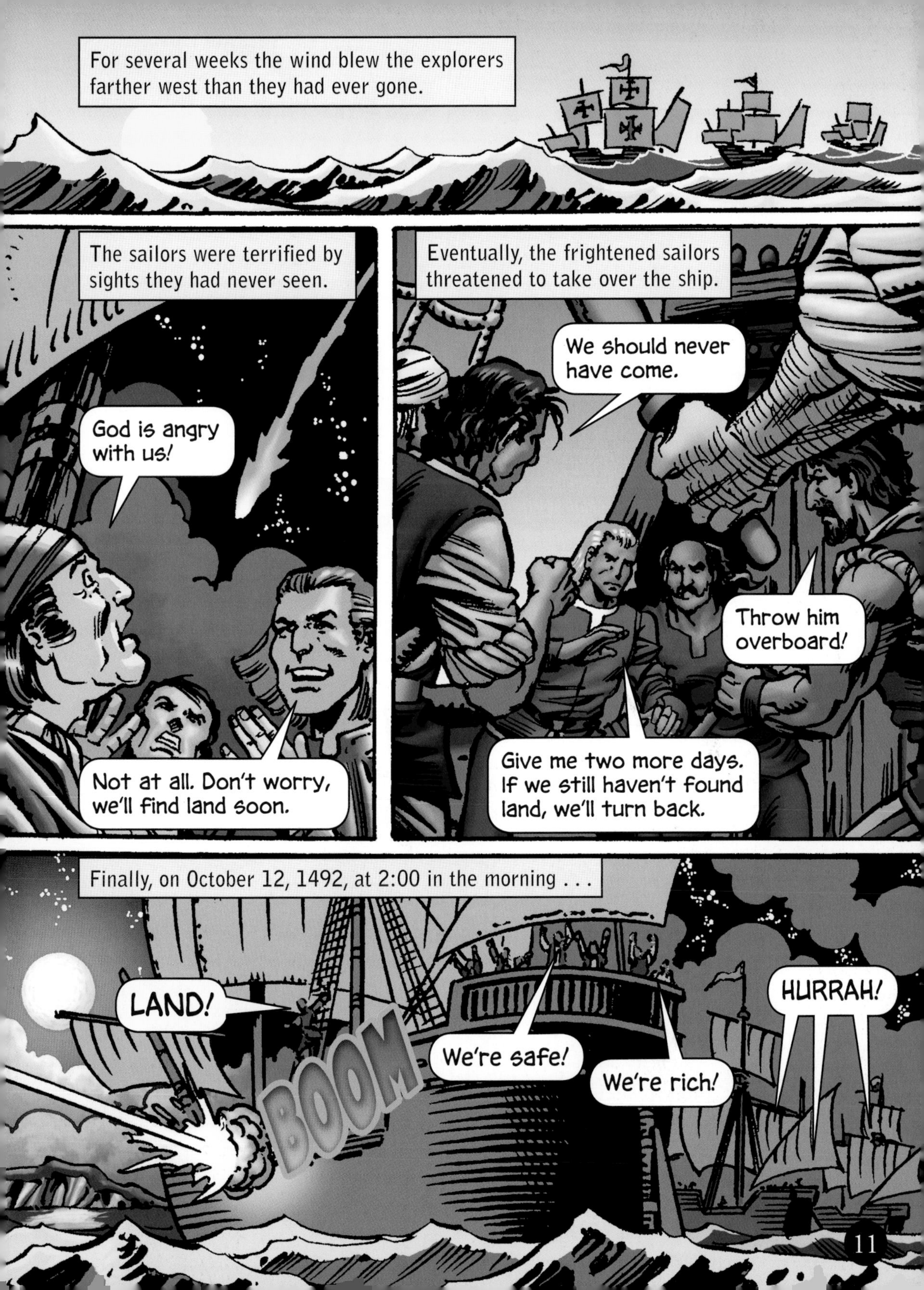
For several weeks the wind blew the explorers farther west than they had ever gone.
The sailors were terrified by sights they had never seen.
God is angry with us!
Not at all. Don't worry, we'll find land soon.
Eventually, the frightened sailors threatened to take over the ship.
We should never have come.
Throw him overboard!
Give me two more days. If we still haven't found land, we'll turn back.
Finally, on October 12, 1492, at 2:00 in the morning . . .
LAND!
BOOM
We're safe!
We're rich!
HURRAH!

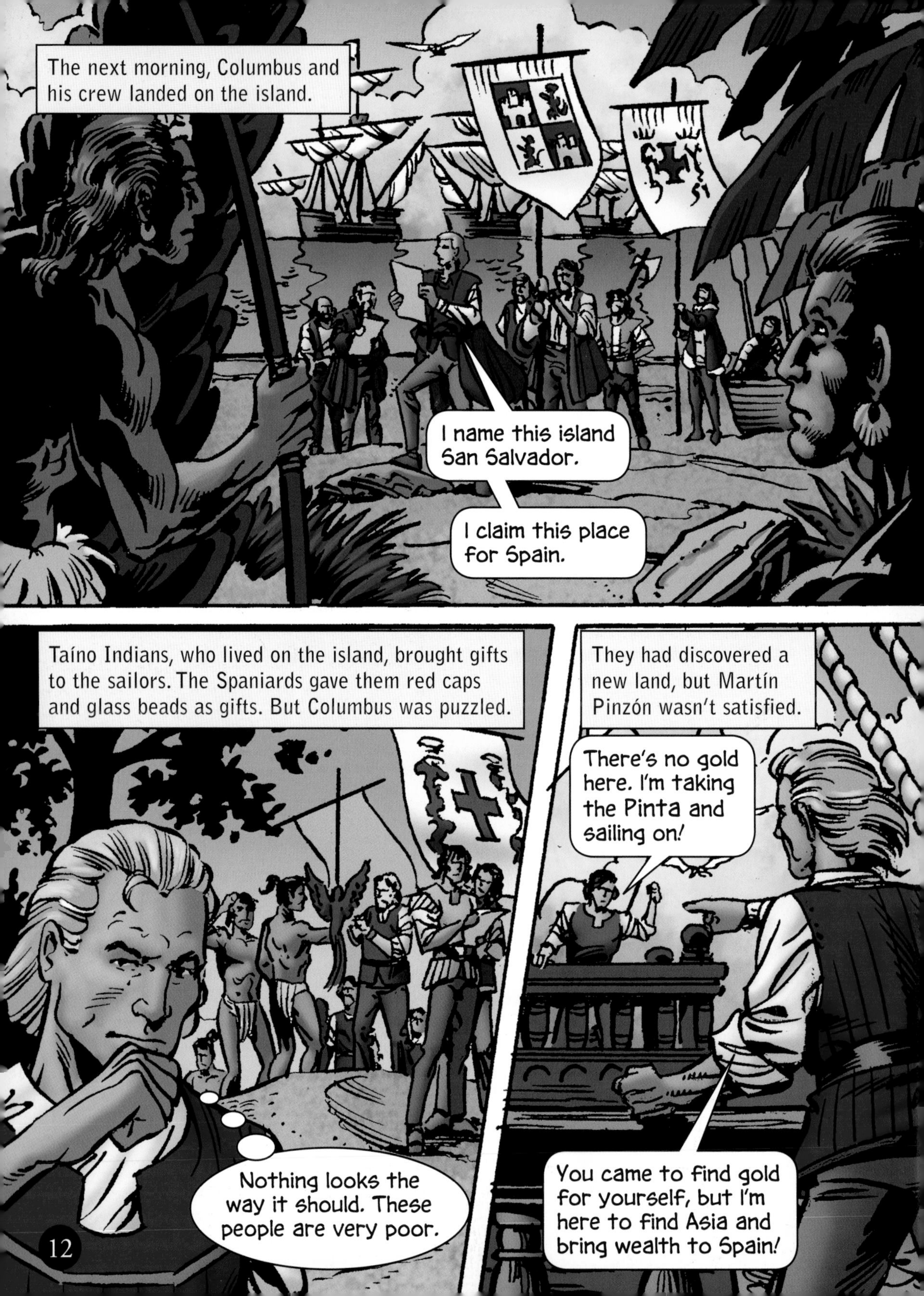
The next morning, Columbus and his crew landed on the island.
I name this island San Salvador.
I claim this place for Spain.
Taíno Indians, who lived on the island, brought gifts to the sailors. The Spaniards gave them red caps and glass beads as gifts. But Columbus was puzzled.
Nothing looks the way it should. These people are very poor.
They had discovered a new land, but Martín Pinzón wasn't satisfied.
There's no gold here. I'm taking the Pinta and sailing on!
You came to find gold for yourself, but I'm here to find Asia and bring wealth to Spain!

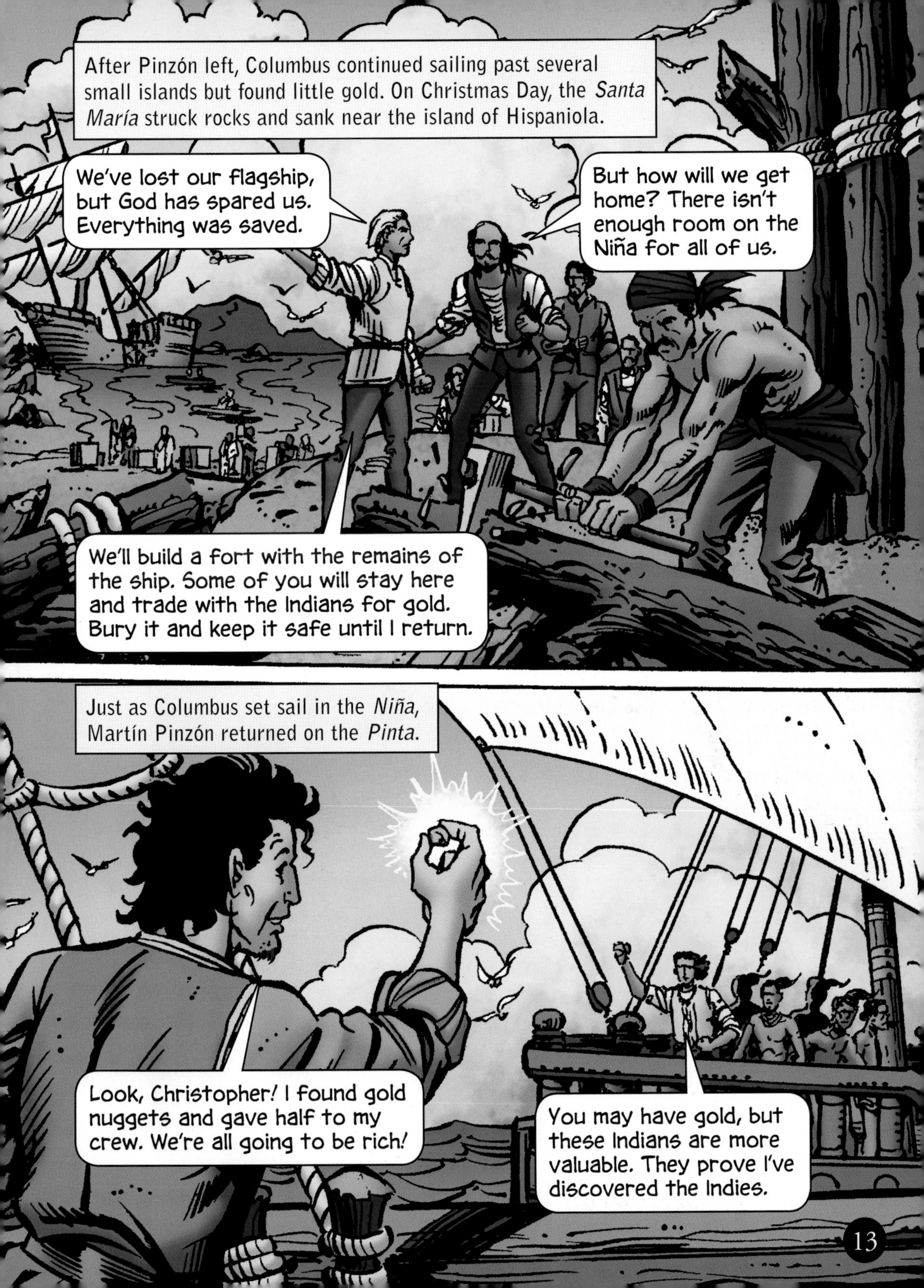
After Pinzón left, Columbus continued sailing past several small islands but found little gold. On Christmas Day, the *Santa María* struck rocks and sank near the island of Hispaniola.
We've lost our flagship, but God has spared us. Everything was saved.
But how will we get home? There isn't enough room on the Niña for all of us.
We'll build a fort with the remains of the ship. Some of you will stay here and trade with the Indians for gold. Bury it and keep it safe until I return.
Just as Columbus set sail in the *Niña*, Martín Pinzón returned on the *Pinta*.
Look, Christopher! I found gold nuggets and gave half to my crew. We're all going to be rich!
You may have gold, but these Indians are more valuable. They prove I've discovered the Indies.

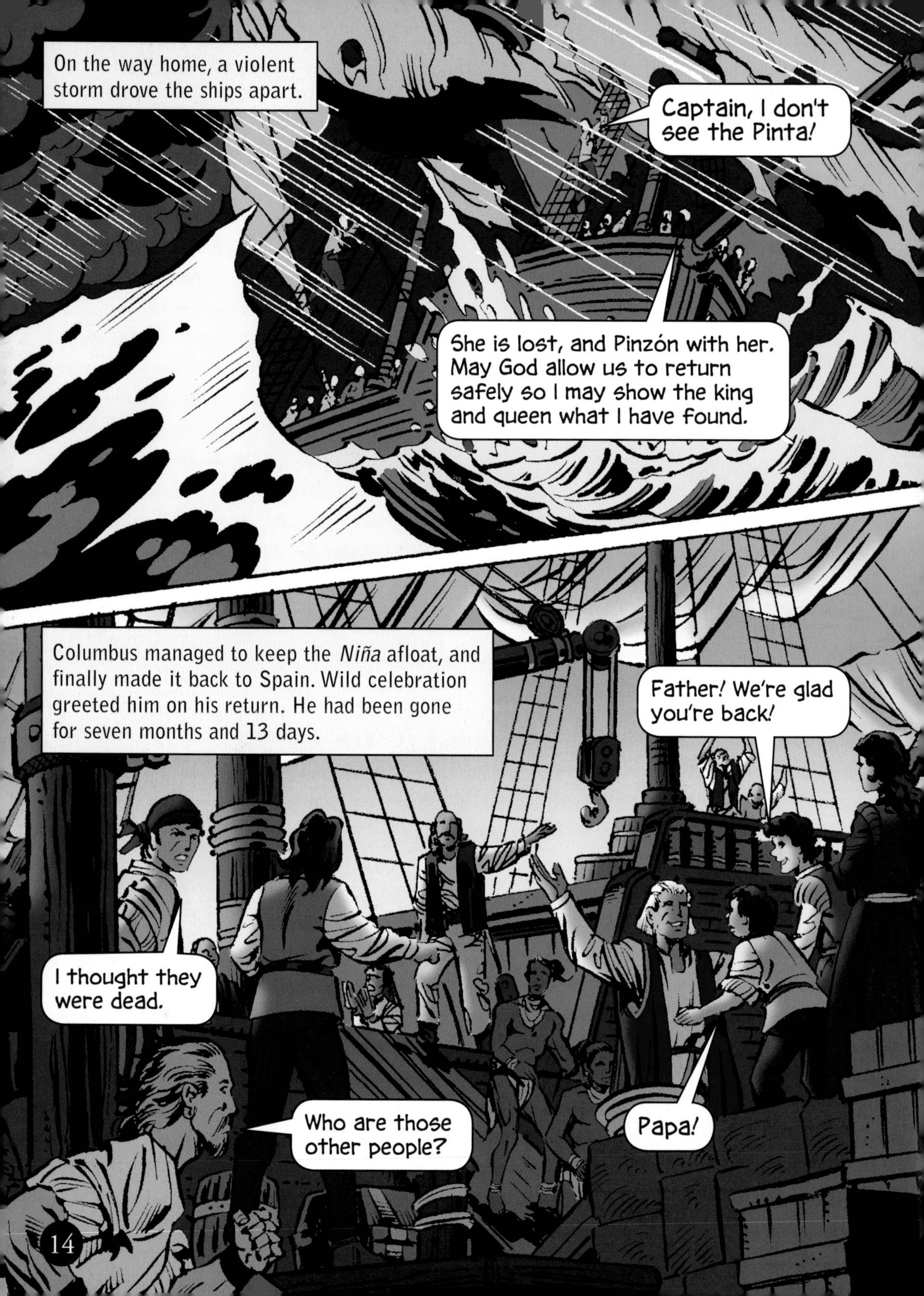

On the way home, a violent storm drove the ships apart.
Captain, I don't see the Pinta!
She is lost, and Pinzón with her. May God allow us to return safely so I may show the king and queen what I have found.
Columbus managed to keep the *Niña* afloat, and finally made it back to Spain. Wild celebration greeted him on his return. He had been gone for seven months and 13 days.
Father! We're glad you're back!
I thought they were dead.
Who are those other people?
Papa!

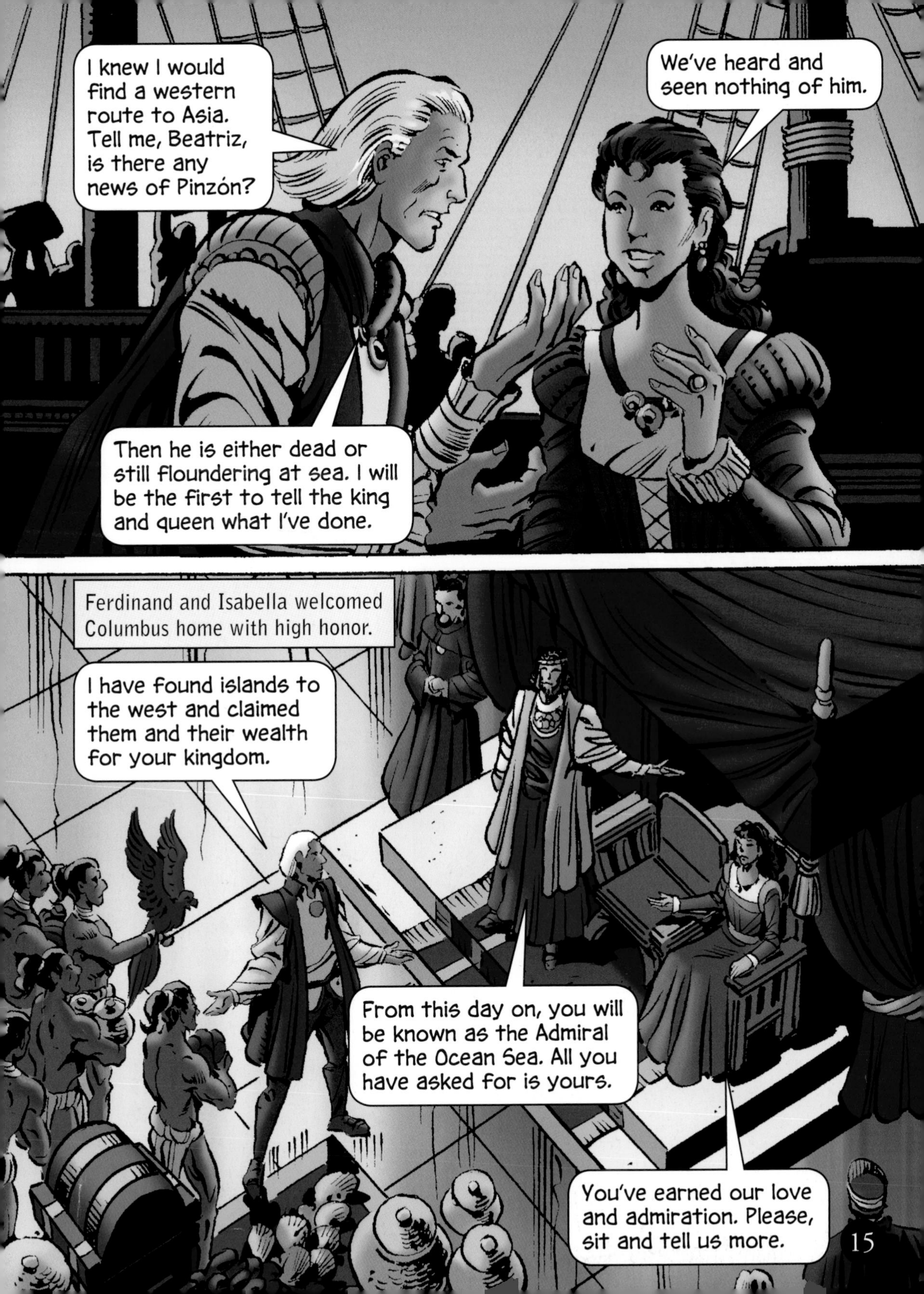
I knew I would find a western route to Asia. Tell me, Beatriz, is there any news of Pinzón?
We've heard and seen nothing of him.
Then he is either dead or still floundering at sea. I will be the first to tell the king and queen what I've done.
Ferdinand and Isabella welcomed Columbus home with high honor.
I have found islands to the west and claimed them and their wealth for your kingdom.
From this day on, you will be known as the Admiral of the Ocean Sea. All you have asked for is yours.
You've earned our love and admiration. Please, sit and tell us more.

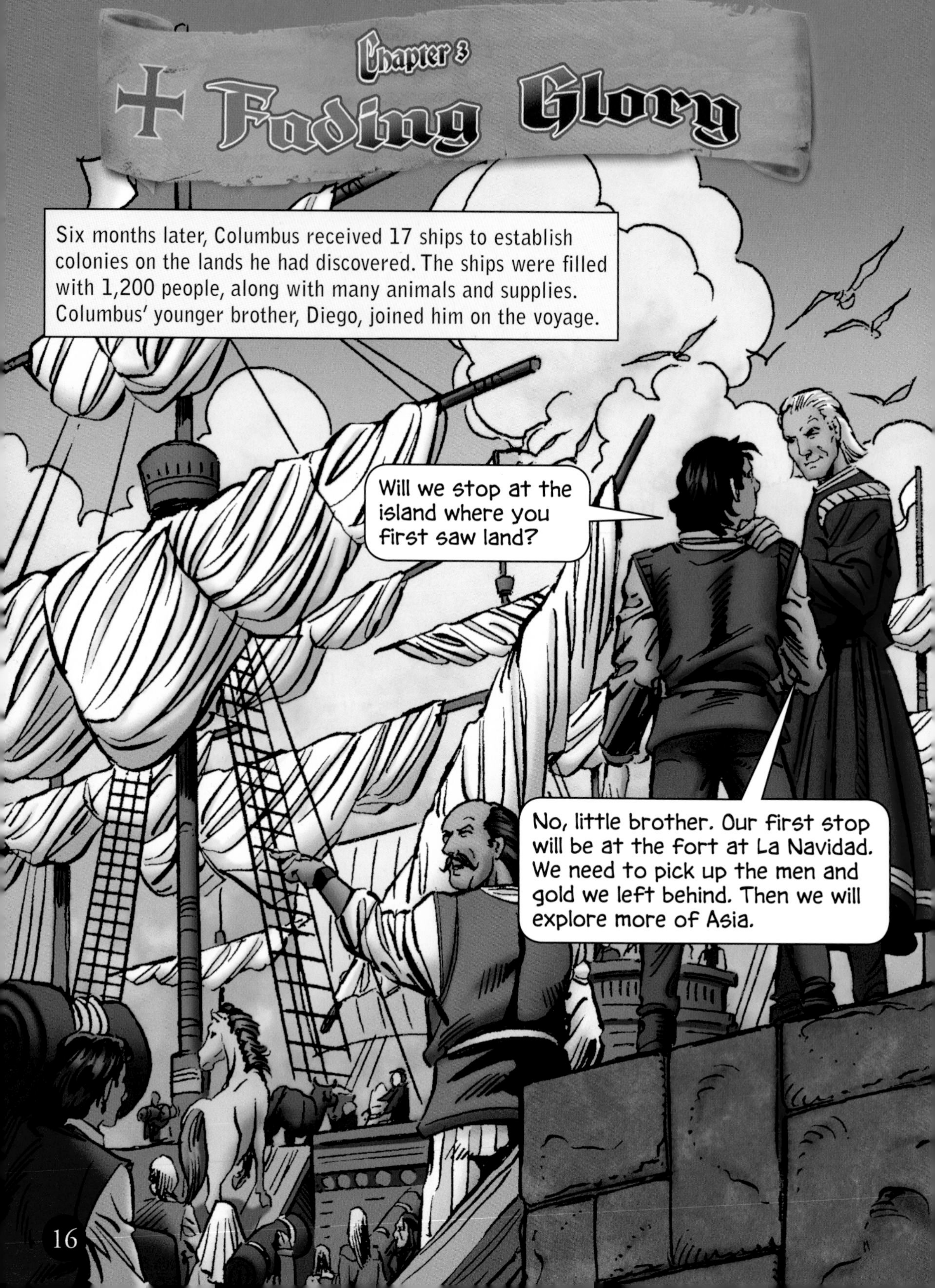
Chapter 3
Fading Glory
Six months later, Columbus received 17 ships to establish colonies on the lands he had discovered. The ships were filled with 1,200 people, along with many animals and supplies. Columbus' younger brother, Diego, joined him on the voyage.
Will we stop at the island where you first saw land?
No, little brother. Our first stop will be at the fort at La Navidad. We need to pick up the men and gold we left behind. Then we will explore more of Asia.

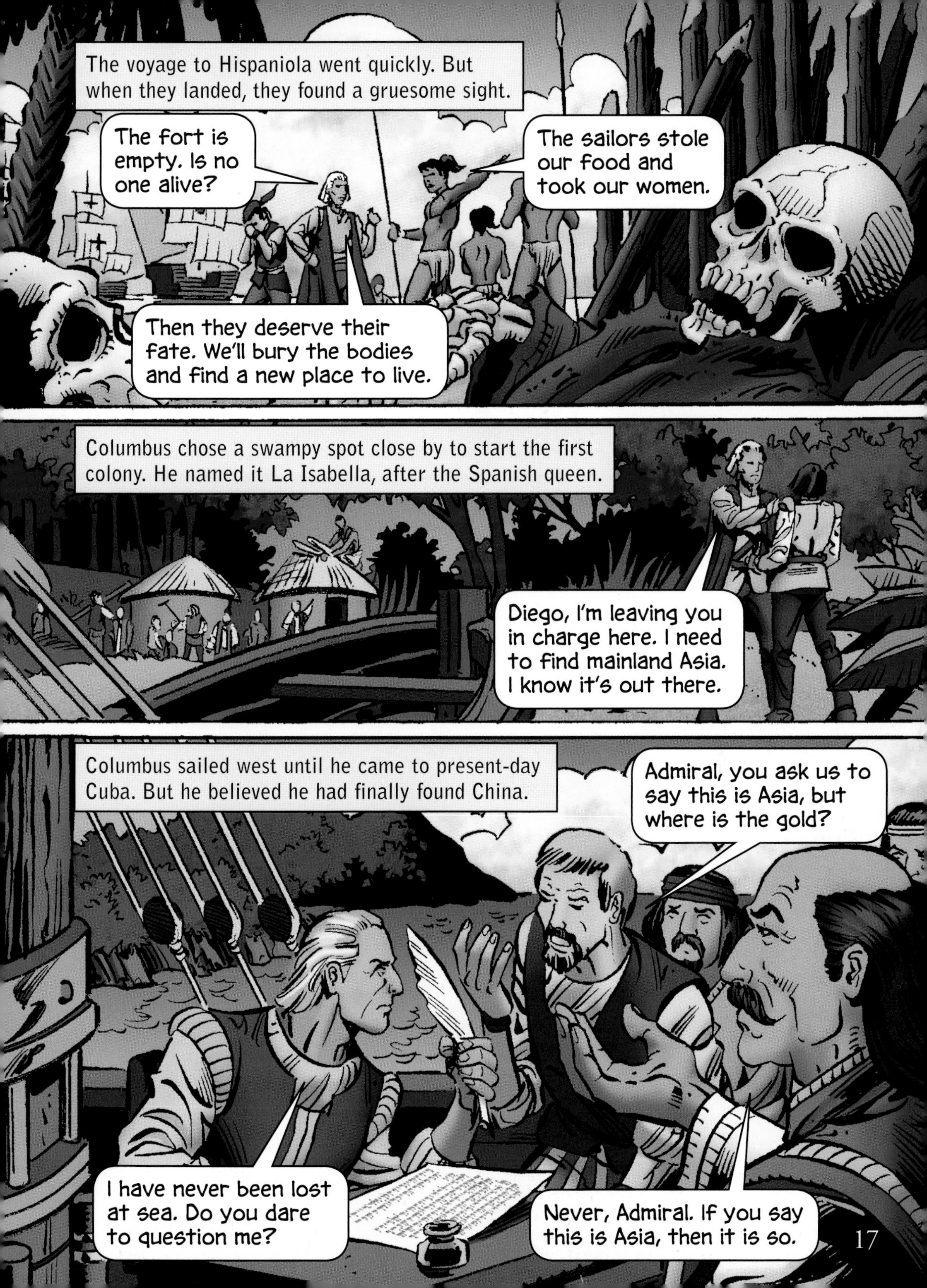
The voyage to Hispaniola went quickly. But when they landed, they found a gruesome sight.
The fort is empty. Is no one alive?
The sailors stole our food and took our women.
Then they deserve their fate. We'll bury the bodies and find a new place to live.
Columbus chose a swampy spot close by to start the first colony. He named it La Isabella, after the Spanish queen.
Diego, I'm leaving you in charge here. I need to find mainland Asia. I know it's out there.
Columbus sailed west until he came to present-day Cuba. But he believed he had finally found China.
Admiral, you ask us to say this is Asia, but where is the gold?
I have never been lost at sea. Do you dare to question me?
Never, Admiral. If you say this is Asia, then it is so.

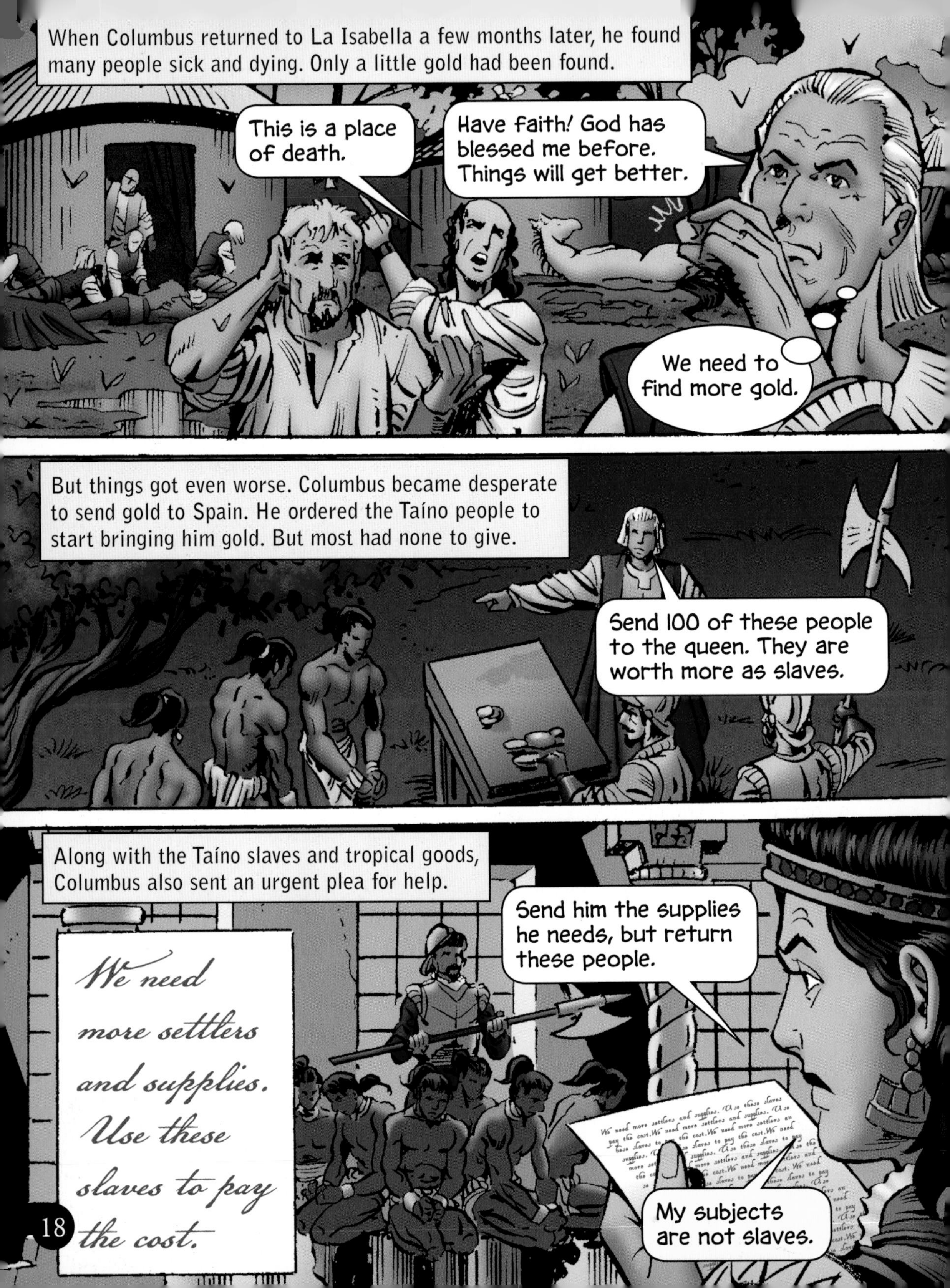
When Columbus returned to La Isabella a few months later, he found many people sick and dying. Only a little gold had been found.
This is a place of death.
Have faith! God has blessed me before. Things will get better.
We need to find more gold.
But things got even worse. Columbus became desperate to send gold to Spain. He ordered the Taíno people to start bringing him gold. But most had none to give.
Send 100 of these people to the queen. They are worth more as slaves.
Along with the Taíno slaves and tropical goods, Columbus also sent an urgent plea for help.
We need more settlers and supplies. Use these slaves to pay the cost.
Send him the supplies he needs, but return these people.
My subjects are not slaves.

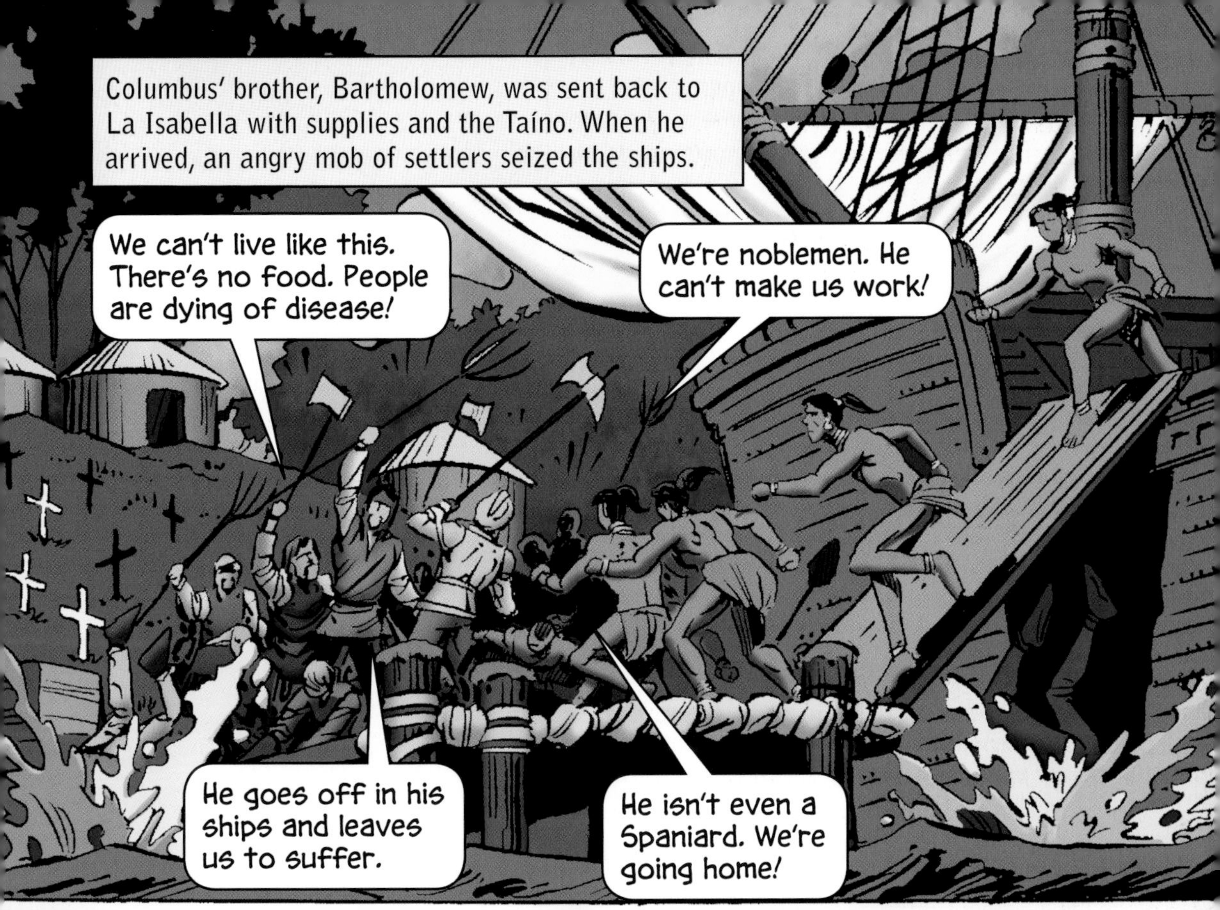
Columbus' brother, Bartholomew, was sent back to La Isabella with supplies and the Taíno. When he arrived, an angry mob of settlers seized the ships.
We can't live like this. There's no food. People are dying of disease!
We're noblemen. He can't make us work!
He goes off in his ships and leaves us to suffer.
He isn't even a Spaniard. We're going home!

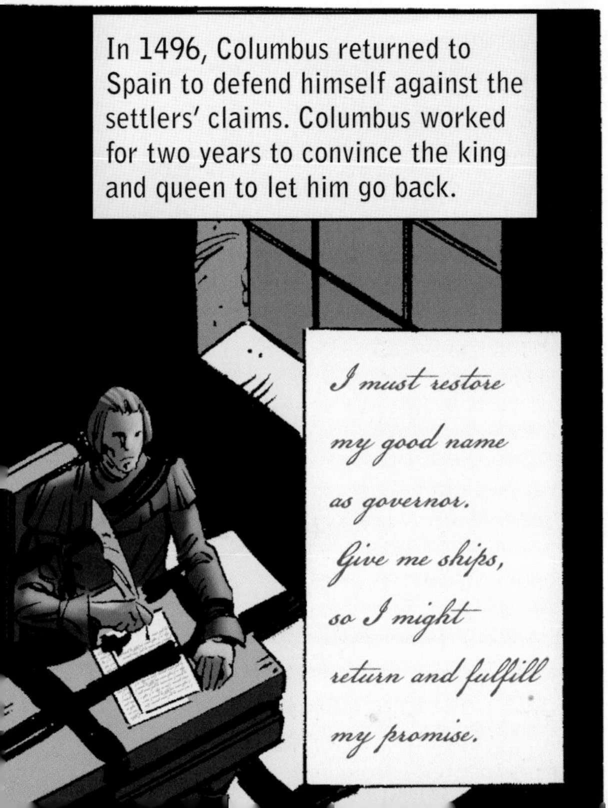
In 1496, Columbus returned to Spain to defend himself against the settlers' claims. Columbus worked for two years to convince the king and queen to let him go back.
I must restore my good name as governor. Give me ships, so I might return and fulfill my promise.

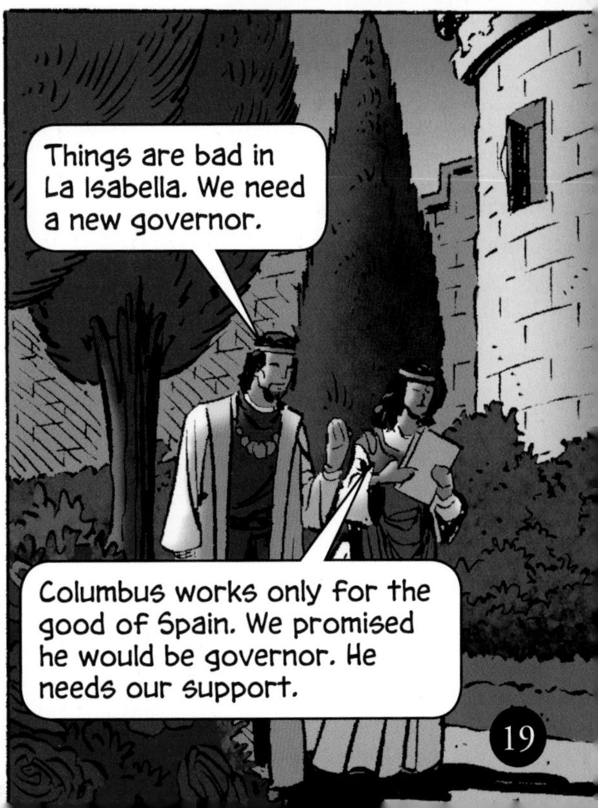
Things are bad in La Isabella. We need a new governor.
Columbus works only for the good of Spain. We promised he would be governor. He needs our support.

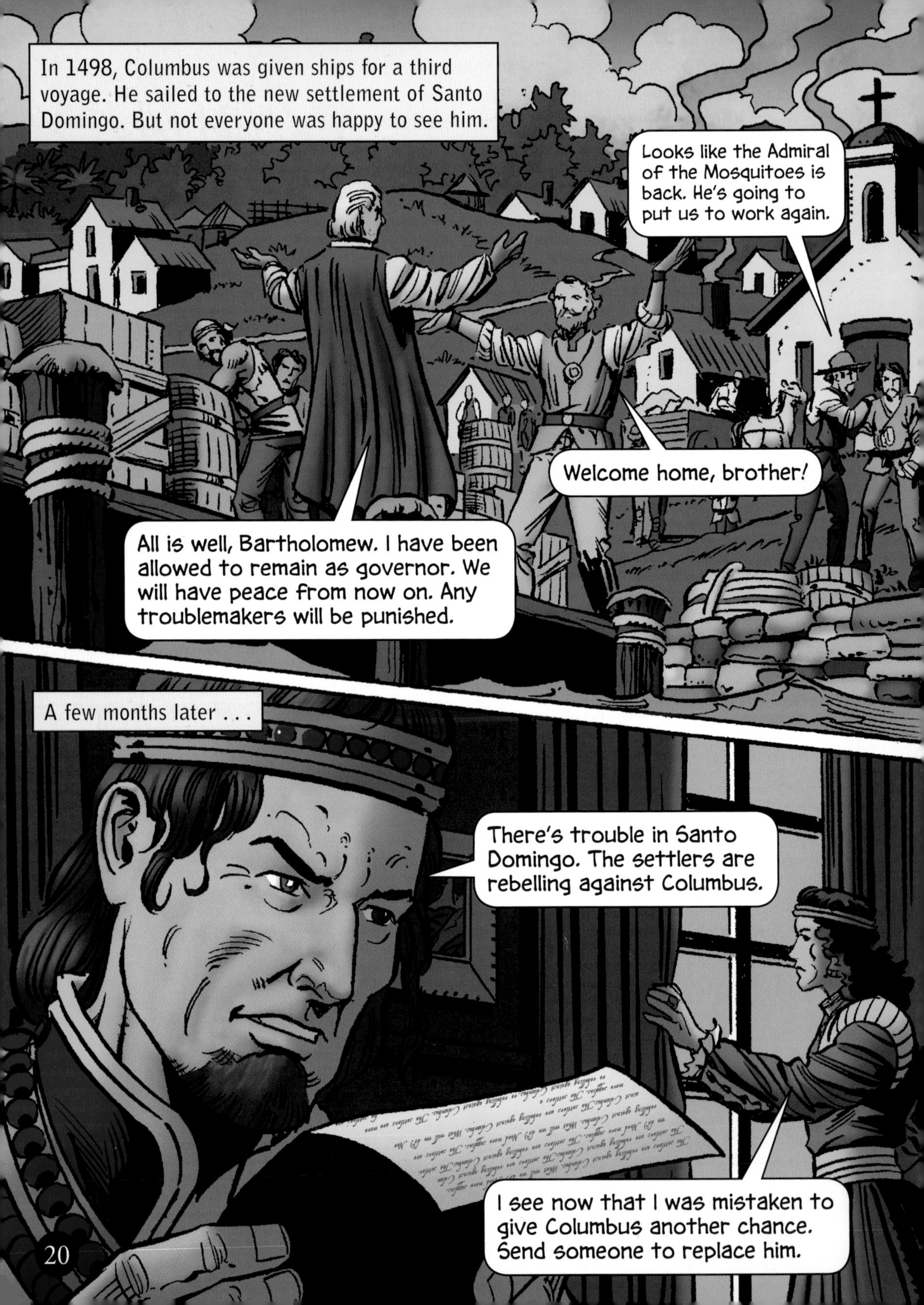

In 1498, Columbus was given ships for a third voyage. He sailed to the new settlement of Santo Domingo. But not everyone was happy to see him.
Welcome home, brother!
All is well, Bartholomew. I have been allowed to remain as governor. We will have peace from now on. Any troublemakers will be punished.
Looks like the Admiral of the Mosquitoes is back. He's going to put us to work again.
A few months later . . .
There's trouble in Santo Domingo. The settlers are rebelling against Columbus.
I see now that I was mistaken to give Columbus another chance. Send someone to replace him.

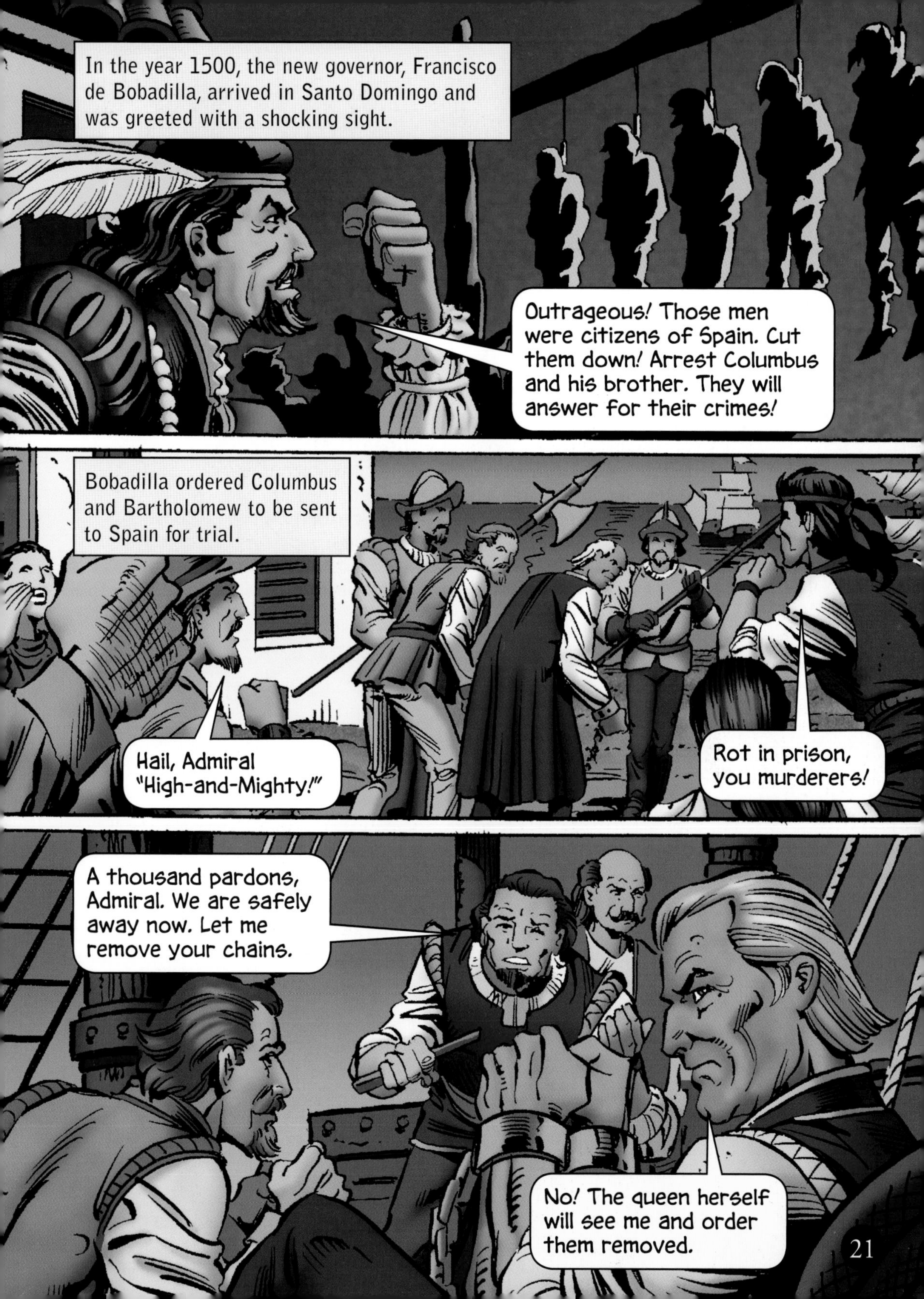
In the year 1500, the new governor, Francisco de Bobadilla, arrived in Santo Domingo and was greeted with a shocking sight.
Outrageous! Those men were citizens of Spain. Cut them down! Arrest Columbus and his brother. They will answer for their crimes!
Bobadilla ordered Columbus and Bartholomew to be sent to Spain for trial.
Hail, Admiral "High-and-Mighty!"
Rot in prison, you murderers!
A thousand pardons, Admiral. We are safely away now. Let me remove your chains.
No! The queen herself will see me and order them removed.

Chapter 4
A Final Voyage

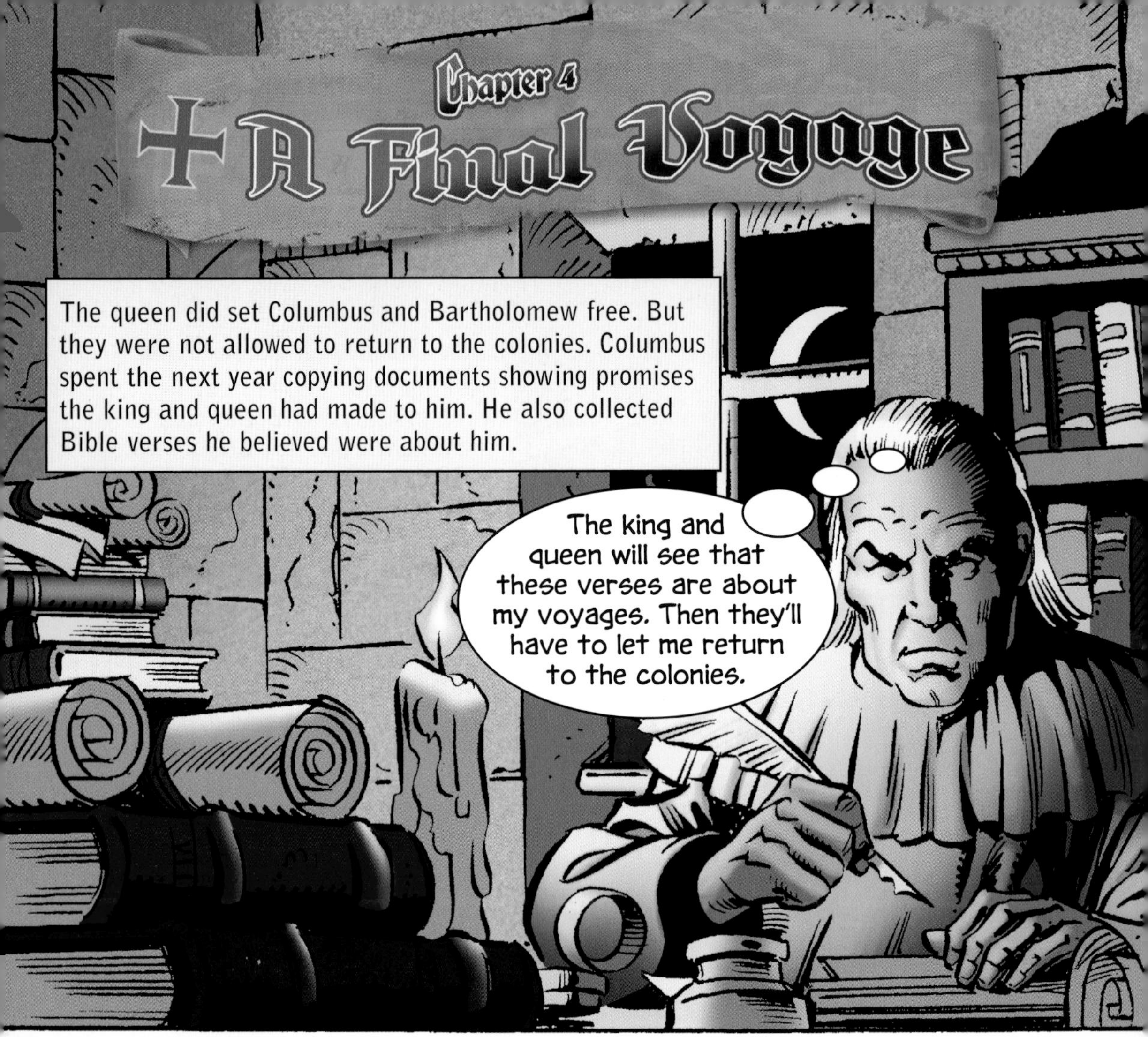

The queen did set Columbus and Bartholomew free. But they were not allowed to return to the colonies. Columbus spent the next year copying documents showing promises the king and queen had made to him. He also collected Bible verses he believed were about him.
The king and queen will see that these verses are about my voyages. Then they'll have to let me return to the colonies.

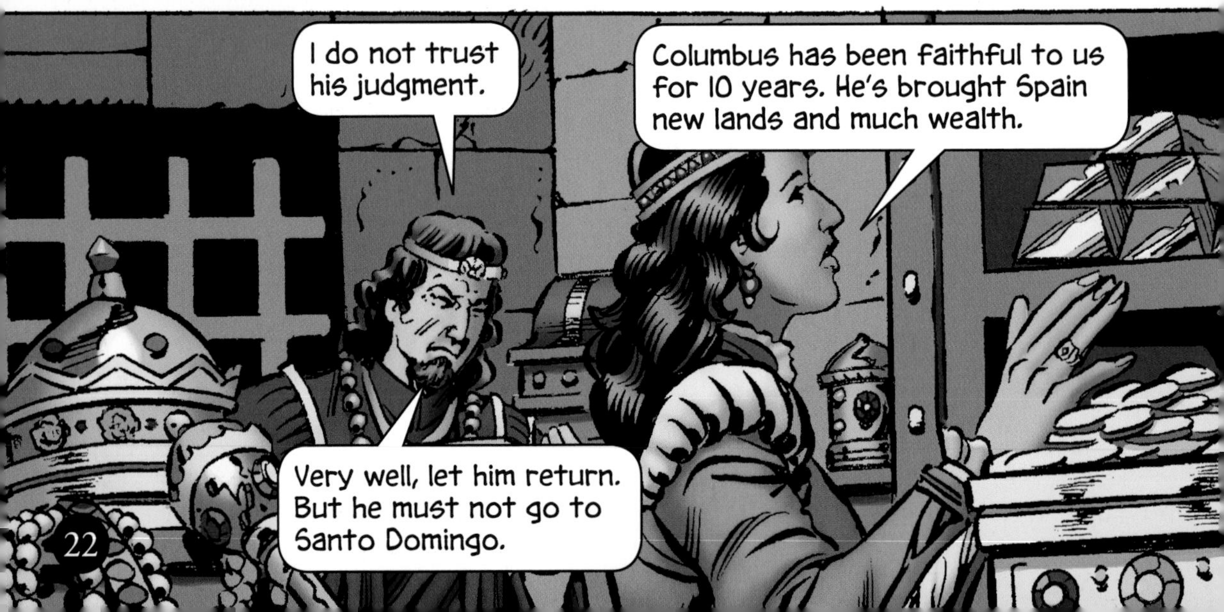

I do not trust his judgment.
Columbus has been faithful to us for 10 years. He's brought Spain new lands and much wealth.
Very well, let him return. But he must not go to Santo Domingo.

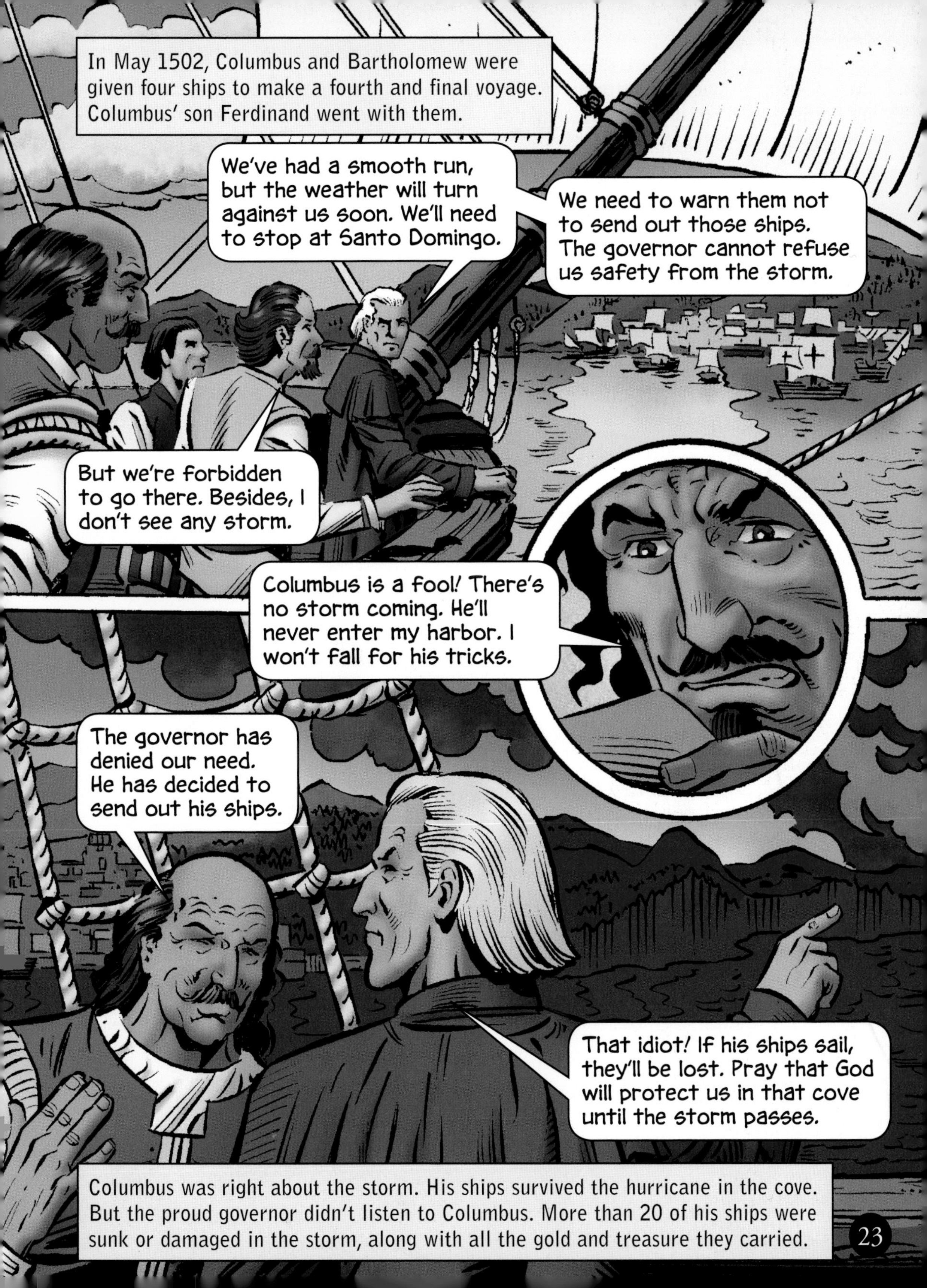
In May 1502, Columbus and Bartholomew were given four ships to make a fourth and final voyage. Columbus' son Ferdinand went with them.
We've had a smooth run, but the weather will turn against us soon. We'll need to stop at Santo Domingo.
We need to warn them not to send out those ships. The governor cannot refuse us safety from the storm.
But we're forbidden to go there. Besides, I don't see any storm.
Columbus is a fool! There's no storm coming. He'll never enter my harbor. I won't fall for his tricks.
The governor has denied our need. He has decided to send out his ships.
That idiot! If his ships sail, they'll be lost. Pray that God will protect us in that cove until the storm passes.
Columbus was right about the storm. His ships survived the hurricane in the cove. But the proud governor didn't listen to Columbus. More than 20 of his ships were sunk or damaged in the storm, along with all the gold and treasure they carried.

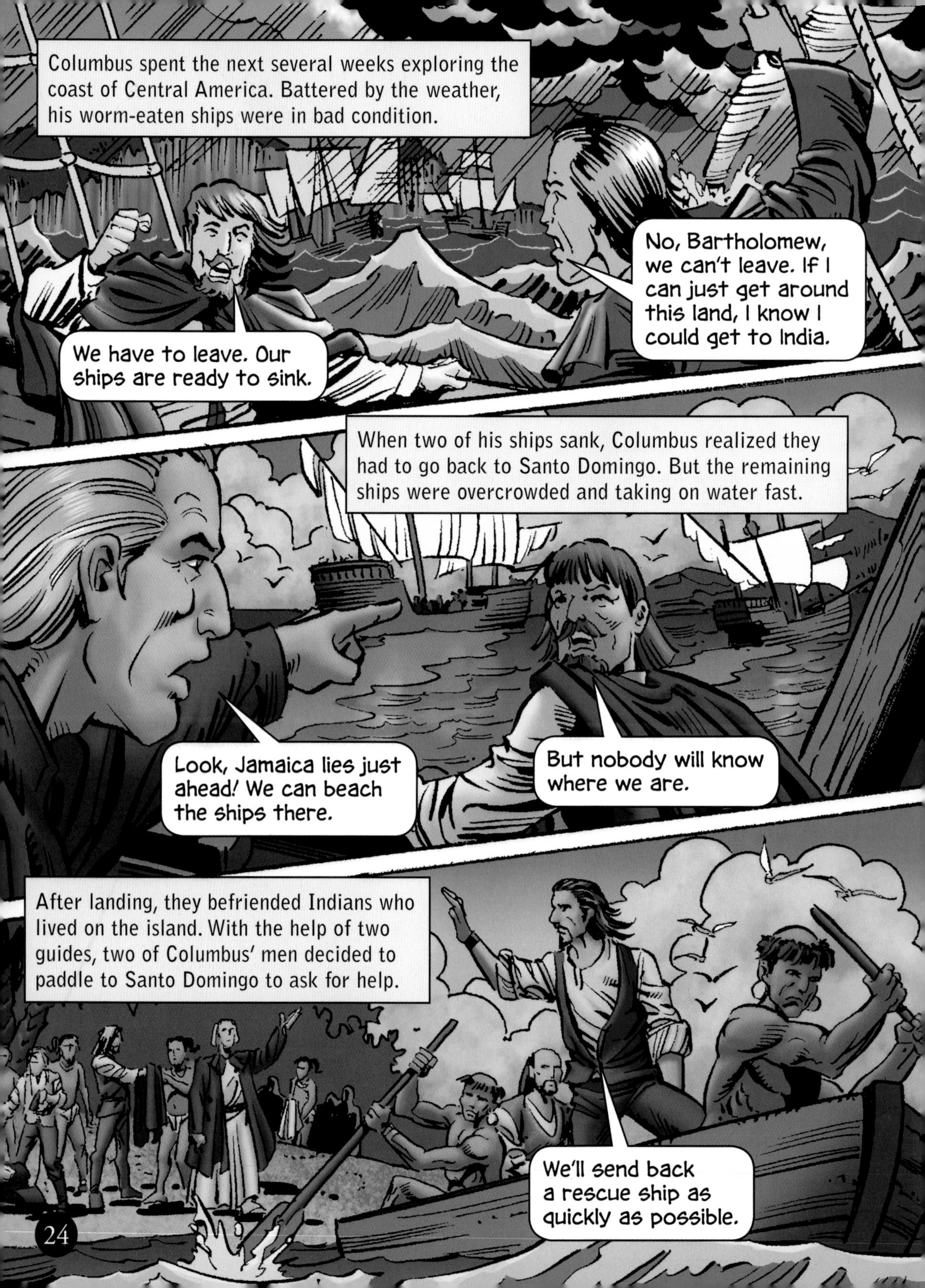
Columbus spent the next several weeks exploring the coast of Central America. Battered by the weather, his worm-eaten ships were in bad condition.
We have to leave. Our ships are ready to sink.
No, Bartholomew, we can't leave. If I can just get around this land, I know I could get to India.
When two of his ships sank, Columbus realized they had to go back to Santo Domingo. But the remaining ships were overcrowded and taking on water fast.
Look, Jamaica lies just ahead! We can beach the ships there.
But nobody will know where we are.
After landing, they befriended Indians who lived on the island. With the help of two guides, two of Columbus' men decided to paddle to Santo Domingo to ask for help.
We'll send back a rescue ship as quickly as possible.

Many months went by with no sign of rescue. The Indians soon grew tired of bringing food to the marooned sailors. But Columbus knew an eclipse of the moon was coming. He formed a plan to trick the natives into cooperating.

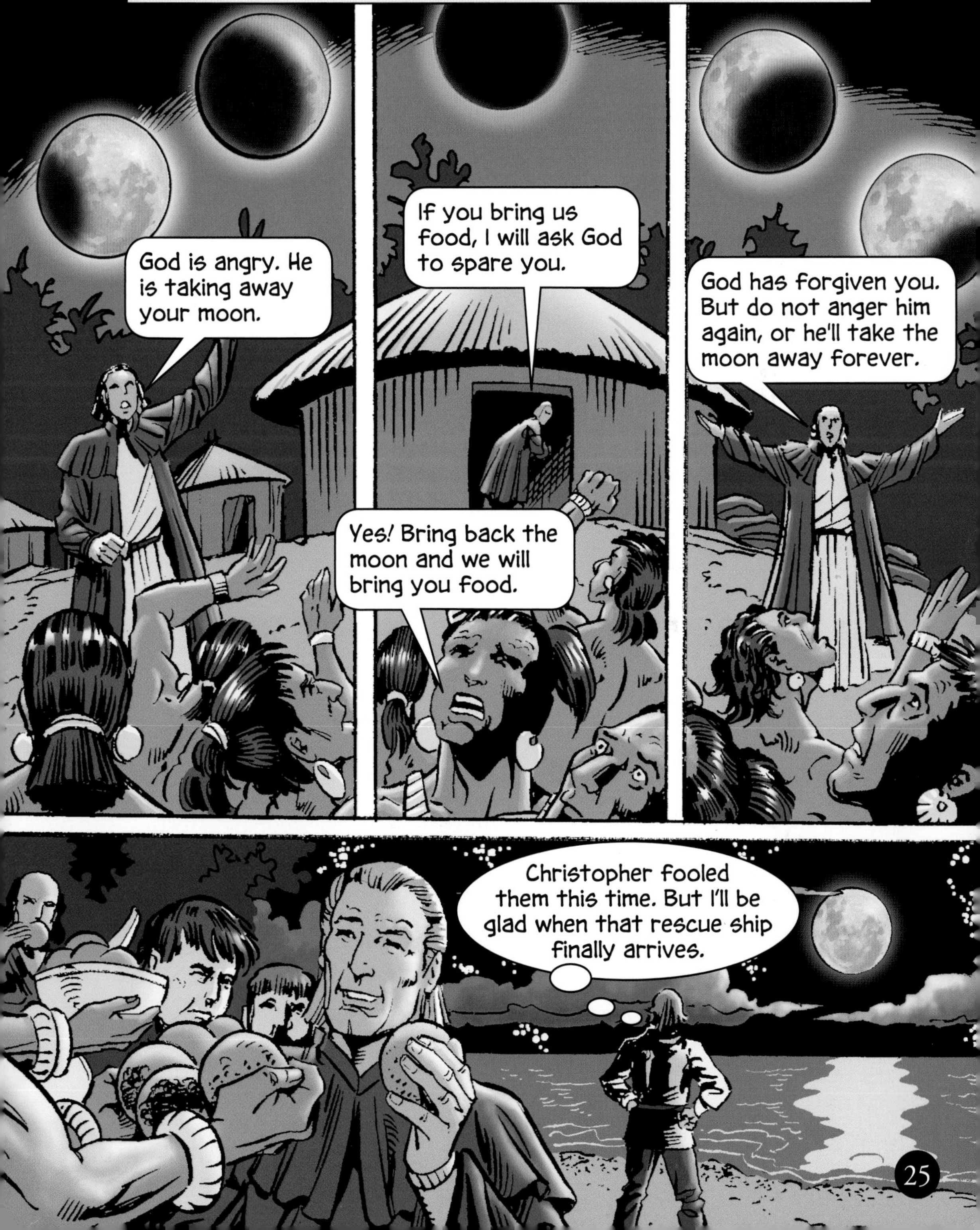
God is angry. He is taking away your moon.
If you bring us food, I will ask God to spare you.
Yes! Bring back the moon and we will bring you food.
God has forgiven you. But do not anger him again, or he'll take the moon away forever.
Christopher fooled them this time. But I'll be glad when that rescue ship finally arrives.

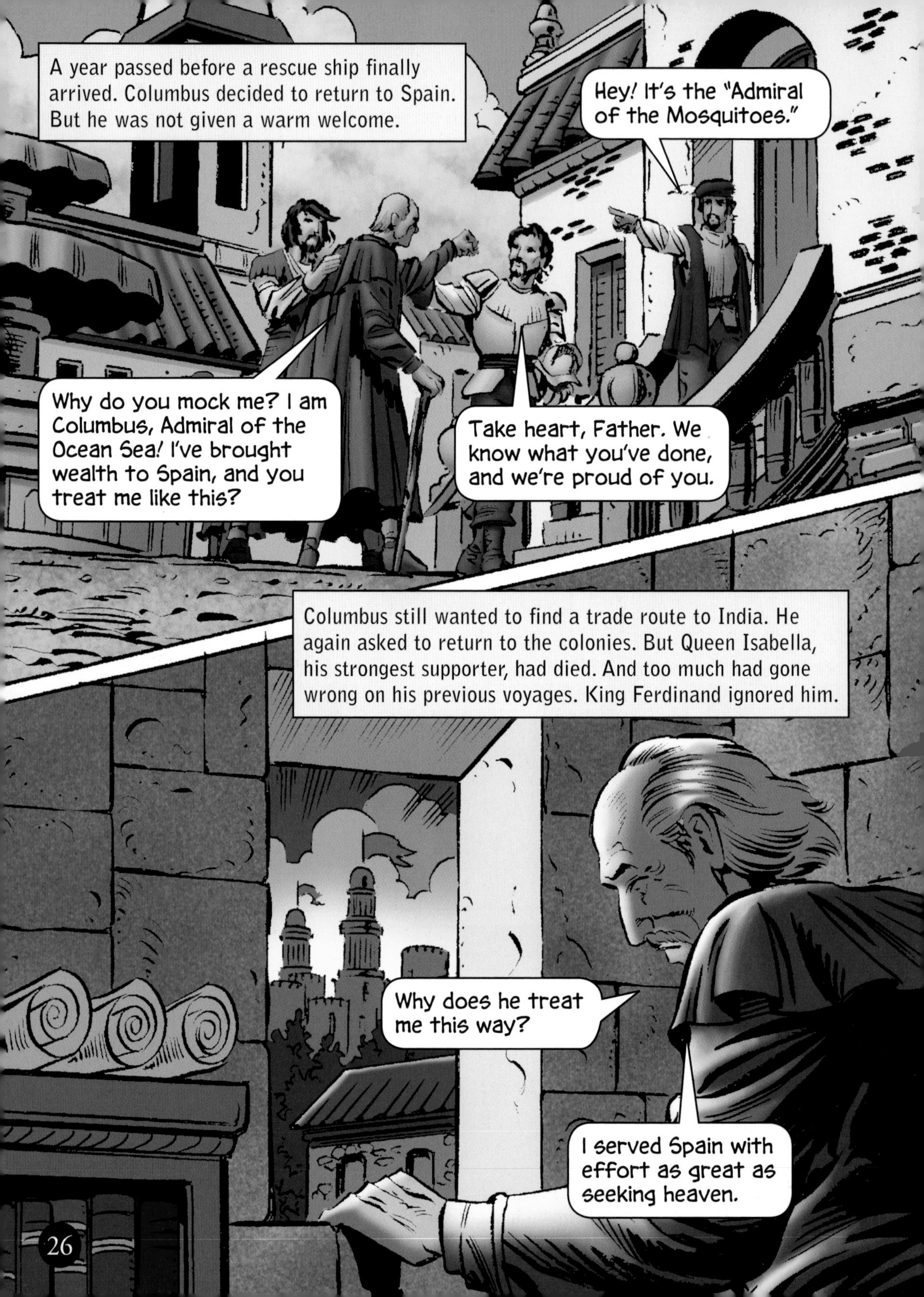
A year passed before a rescue ship finally arrived. Columbus decided to return to Spain. But he was not given a warm welcome.
Hey! It's the "Admiral of the Mosquitoes."
Why do you mock me? I am Columbus, Admiral of the Ocean Sea! I've brought wealth to Spain, and you treat me like this?
Take heart, Father. We know what you've done, and we're proud of you.
Columbus still wanted to find a trade route to India. He again asked to return to the colonies. But Queen Isabella, his strongest supporter, had died. And too much had gone wrong on his previous voyages. King Ferdinand ignored him.
Why does he treat me this way?
I served Spain with effort as great as seeking heaven.

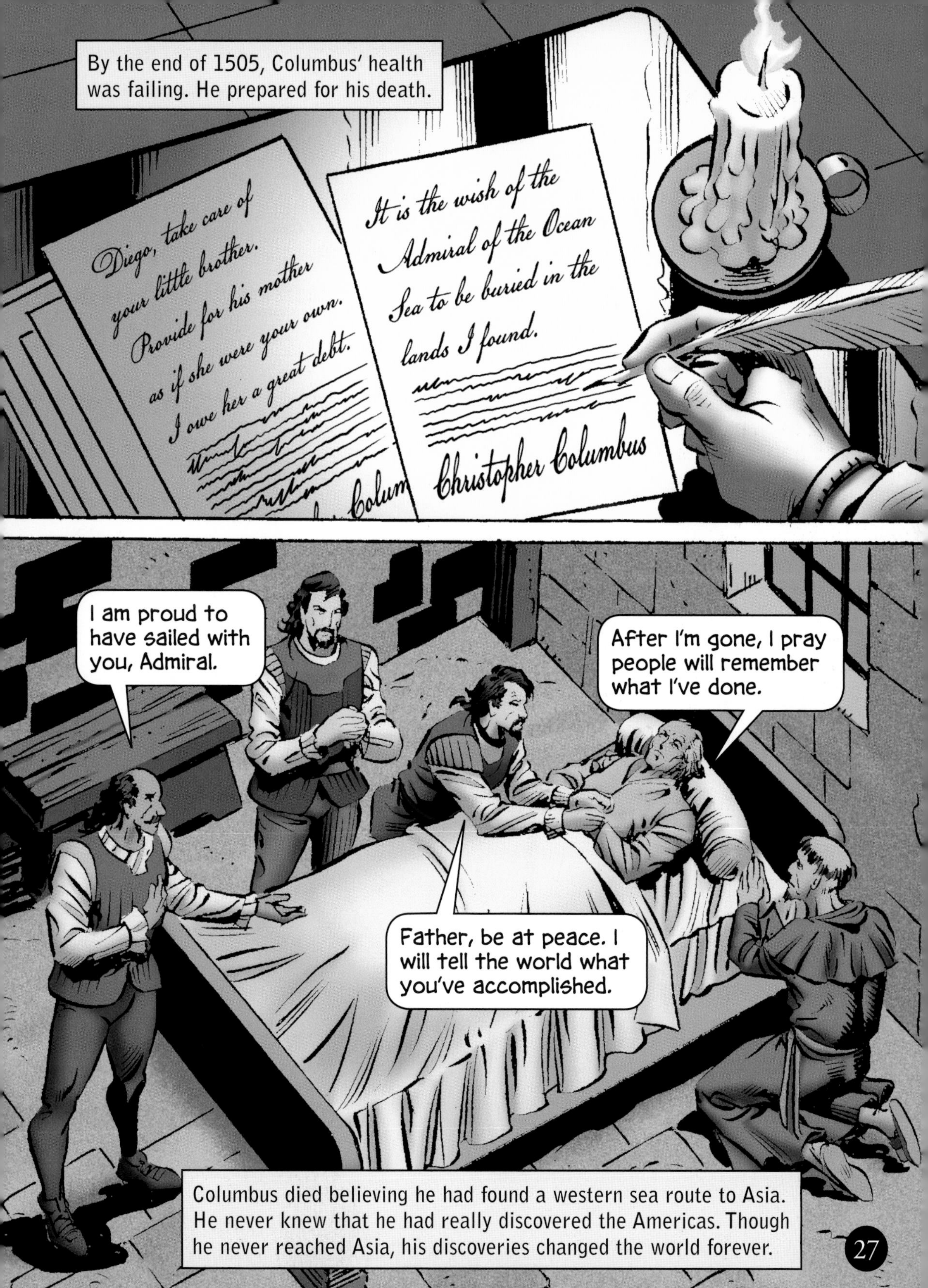
By the end of 1505, Columbus' health was failing. He prepared for his death.
Diego, take care of your little brother. Provide for his mother as if she were your own. I owe her a great debt.
It is the wish of the Admiral of the Ocean Sea to be buried in the lands I found.
Christopher Columbus
I am proud to have sailed with you, Admiral.
After I'm gone, I pray people will remember what I've done.
Father, be at peace. I will tell the world what you've accomplished.
Columbus died believing he had found a western sea route to Asia. He never knew that he had really discovered the Americas. Though he never reached Asia, his discoveries changed the world forever.

More about ☩ Christopher Columbus

☩ Columbus was born in 1451, in Genoa, Italy. He died on May 20, 1506, in Valladolid, Spain.

☩ Though it was the flagship, the *Santa María* was much slower than the *Niña* and *Pinta*. Columbus preferred the *Niña*. The sturdy little ship made three round-trip voyages across the Atlantic Ocean.

☩ Columbus usually sailed by using "dead reckoning." He used a compass to keep the ship moving in the right direction. He measured the distance traveled by noting how fast a floating object passed by the ship. Dead reckoning allowed him to find his way without using landmarks.

☩ Martín Pinzón didn't die in the storm on the return trip from the first voyage. He arrived at Spain only hours after Columbus did. But he died a few weeks later. Vicente Pinzón returned to explore the coast of South America. The Pinzón family later claimed they had a right to part of the newly discovered lands. Their claims were the basis for years of lawsuits. King Ferdinand used these claims to limit Columbus' rights and certain privileges.

✝ No pictures of Columbus were painted during his life. People who knew him said he was tall with a long nose, red hair, and light-colored eyes. His hair turned completely white by the time he was 30 years old.

✝ Ferdinand Columbus became a well-known scholar and wrote a biography about his father's life and discoveries. He also saved many of the notes written by his father, which still exist today.

✝ Columbus made a fifth voyage after he died. In 1537, his body was sent to Santo Domingo. More than 350 years later, Columbus' remains were returned to Spain. But 20 years later, workers in Santo Domingo found a box of bones with Columbus' name on it. Some people think the bones that were taken to Spain were really those of Christopher's younger brother, Diego, who had been made governor of the colony after Christopher died. In 1992, a new monument was built to house the remains of both men. Today, nobody knows which bones are those of Christopher and which are his brother's.

GLOSSARY

colony (KOL-uh-nee)—an area that is settled and ruled by people from another country

hourglass (OUR-glass)—an instrument for measuring time

monastery (MAH-nuh-ster-ee)—a group of buildings where monks live and work

noble (NOH-buhl)—a wealthy, upper-class person of high rank

Taíno (TYE-no)—the tribe of Indians who met Columbus on San Salvador

trade route (TRADE ROUT)—a road or course set up to allow people to exchange goods

INTERNET SITES

FactHound offers a safe, fun way to find Internet sites related to this book. All of the sites on FactHound have been researched by our staff.

Here's how:
1. Visit *www.facthound.com*
2. Choose your grade level.
3. Type in this book ID **0736868534** for age-appropriate sites. You may also browse subjects by clicking on letters, or by clicking on pictures and words.
4. Click on the **Fetch It** button.

FactHound will fetch the best sites for you!

READ MORE

Aller, Susan Bivin. *Christopher Columbus*. History Maker Bios. Minneapolis: Lerner, 2003.

Doak, Robin S. *Christopher Columbus: Explorer of the New World*. Signature Lives. Minneapolis: Compass Point Books, 2005.

Kaufman, Mervyn D. *Christopher Columbus*. Fact Finders. Biographies. Mankato, Minn.: Capstone Press, 2004.

Molzahn, Arlene B. *Christopher Columbus: Famous Explorer*. Explorers! Berkely Heights, N.J.: Enslow, 2003.

BIBLIOGRAPHY

Colón, Fernando. *The Life of the Admiral Christopher Columbus by His Son Ferdinand*. Translated by Benjamin Keen. New Brunswick, N.J.: Rutgers University Press, 1992.

Landström, Björn. *Columbus: The Story of Don Cristóbal Colón, Admiral of the Ocean, and his Four Voyages Westward to the Indies According to Contemporary Sources*. New York: The Macmillan Company, 1967.

Phillips, William D., and Carla Rahn Phillips. *The Worlds of Christopher Columbus*. New York: Cambridge University Press, 1992.

INDEX